The Life of D

MW01153931

TRANSLATED FROM THE ORIGINAL WORK OF
THE VENERABLE SERVANT OF GOD, JOHN BOSCO.

WITH A PREFACE BY
HIS LORDSHIP BISHOP CASARTELLI, Bishop of Salford.

Table of Contents

Preface

"Let us leave a saint to write the life of a saint," is said to have been the exclamation of the Angelic Doctor St. Thomas Aquinas, when he entered the cell of his brother doctor, St. Bonaventure, and found him absorbed in writing the life of his spiritual father, St. Francis.

The peculiar value of the present little book is that it may be said once more to present the spectacle of a saint writing the life of a saint. Only whereas in St. Bonaventure's case a son was writing the life of a father, in this case we have the unique example of a father writing the life of his spiritual son. The writer, the saintly Don Bosco, has already been declared Venerable, and the process for his Beatification is proceeding in Rome.

Little Domenico Savio, whose biography was originally published by Don Bosco very shortly after the holy child's death, was, as will be seen, Don Bosco's spiritual child, and it is a subject of great joy to all his admirers that his cause also has at last been introduced at Rome with the approval of the Holy See.

The publication of this English translation of the life, may, please God, contribute not a little to the successful issue of the cause of his beatification.

There are reasons why the life of Domenico Savio should be considered particularly appropriate at the present day, and also why it should appeal especially to English Catholics.

As will be seen from the narrative which follows, the boyhood of Domenico to some extent coincided with that of our present Holy Father [Pope Pius X], there were less than seven years between the times of their birth, and in many respects the early years of the one were like those of the other.

Both were sons of humble peasant families in the North of Italy; both as boys had to trudge many miles barefooted day by day to attend school; both were distinguished by identical qualities of mind and soul.

More than this. The boy Giuseppe Sarto of Riese was destined to become "the Pope of the Eucharist," and no acts of his wonderful Pontificate have more profoundly influenced the spiritual life of the Catholic Church than his legislation on daily Communion and on the first Communion of children on arriving at the use of reason.

Now it is a remarkable fact that the childhood of Domenico Savio anticipated these profound reforms, inasmuch as, owing to his extraordinary sanctity, he was as early as 1849 admitted to his first Communion at the age of seven, and continued thereafter to be a daily Communicant.

At that date such an event must indeed have appeared phenomenal and seems to constitute Domenico a most suitable patron for the juvenile first communicants and daily communicants of the present discipline.

Nor is this all. Domenico Savio, whom we all hope to see one day raised to the Altars of the Church, died as a schoolboy and when not yet fifteen years of age. He was not a Religious of any Order, he was not a Cleric, nor even as yet a church student, though hoping one day to become one; he was just an ordinary schoolboy, fond of his games, as well as of his books. Herein again we seem to see a peculiarly appropriate patron for all Catholic school children, for Domenico may be truly said to be one of themselves, and in these days of educational strife and danger such a patron is more than ever needed by our Catholic schools.

Last of all we cannot but be struck by the extraordinary fact of Domenico's interest in England, as mentioned in chapter ten, and his wonderful vision narrated in chapter nineteen. As far as I know, there is nothing to show why this little Italian schoolboy should have felt any interest in England, or indeed how he came to know anything about it. It reminds one of the case of St. Paul of the Cross, except that it is a much more wonderful phenomenon in the case of a mere child. For this reason I feel specially pleased to see the life in an English dress, and I sincerely trust that the book may have a wide circulation in English speaking countries, and that all readers, and specially the children of our schools, may join in earnest prayer for the promotion of the cause of one whom we may hope some day to acclaim as "the Schoolboy Saint."

      LOUIS CHARLES
      Bishop of Salford
      St. Bede's College, May 6th, 1914.

Author's Preface

You have frequently asked me to write something about your former companion, Dominic Savio; and now I have done what I could to satisfy your desire. Here is his life, described with that brevity and simplicity which I know is most acceptable to you.

There were two difficulties in the way of publishing this work; first there was the criticism to which one is exposed, who describes what was performed under the eyes of many witnesses. I think I have overcome this by determining to narrate only what has been observed by you or by myself, and which I keep preserved in your own writing.

The other obstacle was the necessity of often mentioning myself, for as Dominic was three years in this House, I must necessarily refer to things with which I am personally connected. This I think I have overcome by adhering strictly to the duty of an historian, which is to present the statement of facts, irrespective of the persons concerned. But if, here and there, I should appear to speak too openly of myself, you must put it down to my regard for the boy who has gone, and for all of you besides; for this affection makes me open my heart to you, as a father does when speaking to his children.

Some of you may wonder why I have prepared a Life of Dominic Savio, and not of other youths who were here at school, and lived lives of eminent virtue. It is quite true that Divine Providence deigned to send us several boys who were examples of holiness, such as Gabriel Fascio, Louis Rua, Camillus Gavio, John Massiglia and others; but the incidents connected with these are not so conspicuous and remarkable as those of Savio, whose whole life was wonderful. However, if God gives me health and grace, I intend to publish a collection of facts concerning these other companions, both to satisfy your desires and my own, and so that you may imitate what may be compatible with your state. In this edition I have inserted several new accounts, which will increase the interest of those who have read the former editions.

But I would ask you to try to draw profit from what I am going to describe; say with St. Augustine: si ille, cur non ego? If a companion of mine, of my age and circumstances, exposed to the same or even greater difficulties, could yet remain a faithful disciple of Christ, why cannot I do the same? Remember that true religion is not a matter of words; there must be deeds. Hence, if you find something related worthy of admiration, do not be satisfied with saying: I like that, or that is very good; but rather say: I want to put into practice what I see is praiseworthy in others.

May God grant you, and all the readers of this book, strength and grace to draw profit from what is therein contained; and may Our Blessed Lady, to whom Dominic was so devout, obtain for us all one heart and mind in serving God, who alone is worthy of being loved above all things, and faithfully served during our whole life.

Chapter I

Early Life and Signs of Extraordinary Gifts.

About ten miles from Turin, in the north of Italy, lies the village of Castelnuovo d'Asti, and there in 1841 lived a good, hardworking couple, Charles and Bridget Savio. About that time, however, there was scarcity of labour in the neighbourhood, and they accordingly moved away in the direction of Chieri, which is about nine miles south-east of Turin; and, having settled at the little township of Riva, Charles Savio applied himself to his trade of an ironworker. On April 2nd of the next year, 1842, a child was born, who was to prove a blessing and consolation to his parents; he was given the name of Dominic at baptism, and though no particular importance was attached to the name at the time, the boy, in later years, held it in particular esteem, as there will be occasion to learn.

When the boy was scarcely two years of age, his parents decided to return to their former neighbourhood, and they settled at Murialdo, which is quite close to their early home at Castelnuovo. Like devoted parents, the careful upbringing of their boy was their chief solicitude, and, considering his tender years, Dominic soon displayed an excellent disposition, and piety seemed to be part of his very nature. Morning and evening prayers at once impressed themselves on his childish mind, and at four years of age he could recite them all quite readily; he was always attentive to his mother's wishes, and only left her to say his prayers in some quiet corner, where he was undisturbed.

In the unreflecting manner, natural to them, children are generally a source of worry and disturbance to their mothers; it is the age when they must touch and examine and often taste everything they come across; but Dominic's parents testify that he never gave the least trouble in this way. He was not only obedient to the smallest point, but ready for any expression of a wish, and tried to forsee opportunities of doing them some little service. He was quite above the average in his appreciation for his parents' kindness, and he had his own method of expressing it, particularly as his father returned from his day's work. He always ran out to meet him, hoped he was not too tired, and promised to pray for him in return for all his labours. So saying, he would enter the house, place his father's chair ready, and attend to all his wants. "This childish appreciation and thoughtfulness," says his father, "were naturally very welcome to me, and as evening drew nigh I began to feel a particular longing to get home, to receive and give these marks of affection; for the boy was everything to me."

Day by day the child's piety increased, and from the time that he was four years of age, there was no need to remind him of his prayers, whether morning or evening or at meals, or at the time of the Angelus; in fact he would even remind others, should they appear to forget them. One day some distraction occurred as they were sitting down to dinner, and grace before meals was forgotten; but little Dominic was too attentive: "Father," he said, "We have not yet asked God's blessing on our food," and he straightway made the Sign of the Cross and began the usual prayer.

At another time a stranger was staying in the house, and he sat down to his meal without any act of religion. Dominic did not like to speak of it openly, yet he was too much moved to remain at the table, and went to one of his quiet corners. When he was questioned about this unusual proceeding by his parents, he replied: "I could not remain at table with one who eats as do the beasts without a thought of God."

Chapter II

Examples of Youthful Virtue at Murialdo. His Early Days at School.

It is a common thing to find people who are incredulous on the subject of youthful piety, and therefore it would be well to state at the outset that, for the following account, the writer is drawing directly from the narrative of the parish priest of the district in which Murialdo lay. In his written account he states:

"Soon after I had been appointed to Murialdo, and had commenced my duties, my notice was drawn in a special manner to a little boy of about five years of age who was brought by his mother to the church. His gentle countenance, his air of composure, his whole demeanour so devout and attractive, drew my attention to him, as they had already drawn the notice of others. When he had learnt the way to church, he would sometimes arrive there before the doors were opened; however, it did not suggest itself to him to spend the interval in play, as doubtless other boys would have done, but he used to kneel down on the steps, place himself in an attitude of prayer and remain thus till the church was opened. Neither rain nor snow seemed to affect him in any way when he was thus occupied. It was therefore very natural that I should be curious to make the acquaintance of this extraordinary child, and I found that he was none other than the little son of the blacksmith, Charles Savio.

If he ever saw me in the street he immediately made a respectful and joyful salutation, and always anticipated my greeting. It was about this time that he commenced to attend the parish school, and his already acquired habits of diligence and of taking pains with everything, soon showed their effect in his rapid progress. He had, of course, to mix with the young and thoughtless boys of his own age, but he always managed to avoid their little quarrels and disputes, although this at times brought upon him taunts and insults, which he bore with remarkable courage and patience. The usual boyish, but by no means praiseworthy, tricks and escapades were part of the usual programme of his companions, but Dominic generally found means for being otherwise employed when these were in progress.

The little habits of piety already described increased with the growing years of his boyhood, and developed in proportion as he had scope for its practice. At five years of age he had already learnt to serve Mass and did so with great devotion. He went in good time every day to the church, and, dearly as he loved to serve, he was ready to yield the privilege to others if they wished to do so, in which case he assisted with great devotion. He often went to Confession, and as soon as he was allowed to make his First Communion he did so with fervour and delight. At the sight of so many signs of unusual piety I often used to think to myself: 'Here surely is a boy of great promise; God grant that some means may be found to bring such rare gifts to maturity.'" . . . Such was the narrative of the parish priest of Murialdo, who had watched over the childhood of this gifted boy.

Chapter III

Dominic is Allowed to Make His First Communion Before the Usual Age. Preparation for the Important Day. His Resolutions.

IT was remarked in the foregoing chapter that Dominic showed exceptional piety when he Approached the Holy Table, but there were important circumstances connected with his First Communion that call for consideration. As far as dispositions are concerned, Dominic appeared to have the most excellent ones; he knew the necessary catechism thoroughly; he had a clear knowledge, considering his years, of this the greatest of the Sacraments, and moreover, his desire to receive it was eager and constant. The only obstacle, therefore, was his age, for at that time, children were usually not allowed to make their First Communion before they were eleven or twelve. Savio was only a boy of seven, and he hardly looked his few years, so that the parish priest hesitated. He consulted the neighbouring priests, and having carefully considered the the boy's knowledge and dispositions, all doubt and hesitation were finally swept aside, and Dominic was allowed to partake, for the first time, of the food of angels.

The boy could not repress his delight when he was told this good news, and a supernatural joy seemed to take possession of his soul. He ran to his mother to tell her; he was eager to spend more time in prayer, or in reading the instructions for Holy Communion; he spent more time than ever at church, before and after Mass; he seemed to be already communing with the angels in adoration. On the eve of the great event in his life, he said to his mother: "As I am going to make my First Communion tomorrow, forgive me the pain I have caused you in the past; from now I shall be much better; I shall be more attentive at school, and more obedient in whatever you tell me to do." His sorrow for what he imagined to be his past faults so moved him as to fill his eyes with tears; and the mother, deeply touched, as was natural, at these pious dispositions in her boy, and remembering that in the past he had been a continual source of consolation to her, comforted him by saying: "Put your fears away, my child, whatever you may have done is all forgiven; pray that God may keep you good, and pray for your father and mother."

When that memorable day dawned, he rose early, and long before the time set off for the church, which he found still shut. He knelt down on the step, as was his wont, and said his prayers, till the doors were opened to admit the children, who by this time had gathered together. There were still some confessions to be heard, so that, allowing for preparation and thanksgiving, and the Mass and discourse, the function of the First Communion was a matter of hours. Dominic had been the first to arrive to offer his salutation to God; he was the last to retire after his thanksgiving. The whole period had been for him one of abstraction from things of earth, and of contact with the things of heaven.

Later on, when any reference was made to his First Communion day, his face would light up with joy, as he exclaimed: "That was indeed a day of happy remembrances for me:" It was a sort of re-commencement of a life which might serve as a model to all. In his little book of devotions he wrote down some resolutions, which I have been able to transcribe with all their original and direct simplicity, and their introduction in diary form:

"Resolutions made by me, Dominic Savio, in the year 1849, on the day of my First Communion, at the age of seven.

1. I will go to Confession often, and as frequently to Holy Communion as my confessor allows.
2. I wish to sanctify the Sundays and festivals in a special manner.
3. My friends shall be Jesus and Mary.
4. Death rather than sin.

These resolutions were not simply written out and then put carefully away; he read them very often, and they were a guide to him throughout his life.

If among the readers of this little work there should chance to be some who are yet to make their First Communion, I would strongly urge them to follow young Savio as their model. But in particular, fathers and mothers, and those who exercise any authority over the young, should attach the greatest importance to this religious act; for a First Communion that is well made constitutes a solid moral foundation for the whole future life; and it would be indeed surprising if this solemn act, when worthily performed, did not result in a virtuous life.

On the other hand, great numbers of young people are met with, who are the despair of their parents and of those who interest themselves in them;the root of this evil is generally found to lie in the fact, that their preparation for First Communion was carelessly conducted, or in great part neglected. It would be better to delay it, or even not to make it at all, than that it should be made badly.

Chapter IV

Dominic's School Career at Castelnuovo d'Asti. Trials and Difficulties.

As his early studies were now completed, Dominic should have been sent away to a higher school for more advanced classes, which a small country place could not provide. He was very desirous that this should be arranged, and his parents were greatly in favour of it, but their condition did not allow of the realisation of such ambitious plans. Divine Providence, however, intended to provide the means, so that the boy might attain the end appointed for him.

Dominic had often said in his playful manner: "If I were a bird I should like to fly every morning to Castelnuovo d'Asti so as to go on with my studies."

His eager desire to continue his studies made overcome all difficulties, and it was arranged that he should attend the Municipal schools, although they were two miles away from his home. He had to walk there and back; he was not yet ten years of age, and all the variations of weather, both for summer and winter, had to be put up with; but all difficulties were to be overcome; Dominic was satisfied that he was thus performing an act of obedience to his parents which meant advancing in the science of the Saints, and this appeared to him more than enough reason for putting up with any inconvenience.

One day an elderly person saw Dominic going along the road, about two o'clock in the afternoon, under a broiling sun, and, meaning to give him a little encouragement, said to him: "Are you not afraid to go so far alone?"

"I am not alone," said Dominic, "I have my angel guardian with me, accompanying every step."

"But surely you find the journey long and tiresome in this very hot weather."

"Nothing seems tiresome or painful when you are working for a master who pays well."

"And who is your master?"

"It is God, our Creator, who rewards even a cup of cold water given for love of Him."

This little incident was related by the person who had the conversation with Dominic, and he concludes by saying: "A boy who has such thoughts in his head, when he is only ten years old, is certainly destined for some great career."

At school Dominic soon found how to distinguish between desirable companions and those whose influence was bad. If he noticed one who was diligent and respectful, who knew his lessons well, and always worked hard, Dominic sought his companionship; an unruly, insolent boy, or one who neglected his work, he left severely alone. He was always kindly in his manner towards them, and seized any opportunity of doing them a little service, but he took care not to become intimate with them.

His conduct at the higher school of Castelnuovo d'Asti might serve as a model to any young student who desires to advance in knowledge and virtue. For this reason, the account given by his master is useful and noteworthy. He says:

"I very willingly send you an account of Dominic Savio, because in a very short time he gained a high place in my estimation and affection, and because I still have a vivid recollection of his excellent behaviour, his zeal in good works and his many virtues. I cannot say much about the performance of his religious duties, for he attended the parish church of his own district, which was two or three miles from the school; for that reason he did not belong to our confraternity, though he was just the sort of boy we should have been glad to admit.

He came to this school as soon as his elementary course was over, beginning on the feast of St. Aloysius, June 21st, 1852. That was, in itself, a little extraordinary, for the great patron of young students found no more devoted follower than Dominic. He was gentle in appearance and manner, and had an air about him of mingled gravity and affability. His disposition was always marked, by calmness and good nature; both in school and out of it, his conduct was such as to produce a most agreeable impression, and for me to deal with him in the course of his school work was like a reward for the many fatigues so often to be endured in the training of boys, who are often dull and not eager for lessons. Hence it may very well be said that he was Savio (wise), not only in name, but in fact, viz., in his studies, in piety, in conversation and his dealing with others, and in all his actions.

From the day he entered the school to the end of that scholastic year, and during the four months of the next year that he spent with us, his progress in his studies was little short of phenomenal. He speedily gained the first place in his class, and the other honours of the school, and invariably got full marks for the subjects which were examined from time to time. These eminently successful results must be attributed to his exceptional abilities and to his love of study and virtue.

Deserving also of special praise was his exactness in every duty, no matter how trivial, and his constant attendance at the classes, in spite of all difficulties and of his long walk to the school. He was by no means a robust or vigorous boy, and this going to and from school, a distance of nearly three miles each way, would in itself be ample proof of his assiduity in his studies. But during that year, 1852-1853, he showed signs of weakness and general failing health, so that his parents decided on a change of abode. I was disappointed at losing so promising a pupil, too whom I had become attached, but I had expected to lose him, for I had seen that his delicate constitution was beginning to give way under the strain; and when I heard later on that he was to go to the Oratory at Turin, I was quite satisfied, as I knew he would there have the opportunity for the cultivation of his rare intellect and piety."

Such is the account given by the master of his class.

Chapter V

Dominic's School-Life at Mondonio. His Conduct Under a Calumnious Charge.

It would seem that Divine Providence had designed to make it clear to Dominic that this world is truly a land of exile, where, like pilgrims, we are always moving from place to place; or it may have been that it was in order to make him known in several districts, that his virtues might be displayed in each.

As has been mentioned, it was towards the close of the year 1852 that Dominic's parents found that their boy's health would necessitate another change of abode, and this time they went to Mondonio, a village not far away from Castelnuovo. Here again we find that nothing but the most edifying reports are given of Dominic. It will not be necessary to quote a full account given by his master at Mondonio, for it repeats the good points mentioned by his former master at Murialdo. Attention will be drawn only to certain facts of particular importance.

The priest in question, writes: "I can state, without hesitation, that during my twenty years experience with boys I never met one to equal Savio in frank and genuine piety. He was gifted, with a wisdom beyond his years; and his diligence, application and affability, made him a favourite both with masters and companions. When I noticed him in church his recollection was such as to fill me with wonder; his manner and attitude suggested the thought: "Here is an innocent soul to whom the delights of heaven are opened, and who by his piety soars aloft to the company of the angels in Heaven."

The following incident is worthy of special record:

"One day a serious offence had been committed by certain pupils of mine, and the guilty ones, when found, were to be expelled. The culprits thought out several expedients in order to escape the punishment, and at last settled on the plan of accusing Dominic of the offence. I very naturally refused entirely to believe that Dominic would be capable of any such thing, but the story and accusation were so skilfully put together, that it had all the semblance of truth and conviction.

When I entered the school in the morning, prepared to deal with the matter, I was in an indignant frame of mind, and spoke in general terms to the class. Then I turned to Savio and spoke very severely to him, telling him that he deserved to be expelled, and it was only because it was the first offence he had been guilty of, that he would not be sent away; but that if ever the like occurred again, expulsion would certainly follow. Dominic might have very easily shown that he was entirely innocent, but he made no reply. He hung down his head, as one who was deservedly reproved, and made no attempt at clearing his character.

But it is seldom God's way to let the innocent remain under the cloud of calumny, and on the very next day the culprits were discovered. Deeply regretting now the harsh terms of the reproof I had made to the boy, I sent for him and said: "Why did you not tell me that you had had nothing to do with it?" He replied in his usual candid manner: "I knew that the guilty boy was already under threat of expulsion for other things, but I hoped to be forgiven, since it was the first act of misconduct ever imputed to me at school. I also remembered that Our Lord had been unjustly accused:"

At this reply I was silent; I somehow felt that there was nothing more to be said; not only the masters, but the whole school admired this act of generous resignation to suffering and insult on behalf of others, especially at the risk of being humiliated and disgraced.

Chapter VI

My First Meeting with Dominic Savio. Some Curious Incidents Connected With It.

The matter contained in the following chapters is based upon more personal and complete evidence, for almost all the incidents occurred under my own notice, and also in the presence of a large number of boys who are unanimous in their attestation of them.

It was in 1854 that Fr. Cugliero, the priest who relates the incidents mentioned in the foregoing chapter, came to see me about a pupil of his. "Here in your Oratory," he said, "there might possibly be boys equal to him, but I can safely assert that there is none to excel him; in fact you find him to be another St. Aloysius."

At that time I used to take my boys occasionally to Murialdo. It was a little country place, where a short time was spent for the benefit of enjoying the country air and open life; and there we usually made the Novena in preparation for, and celebrated the Feast of the Holy Rosary. It was accordingly arranged that while I was at Murialdo, Dominic should be brought over from Mondonio to see me.

It was therefore at Murialdo, on the first Monday in October 1864, that I became acquainted with Dominic Savio. He was accompanied by his father, and as they came up to speak to me, I noticed his pleasant, but respectful manner, and something in his demeanour fixed my attention upon him. When he came up I put a question to him, to which he answered: "I am the boy of whom Fr. Cugliero has spoken to you. I have come with my father from Mondonio."

We walked together and I questioned him about his studies, and his desires for the future, and we were immediately on the most friendly and confidential terms. I may say that I at once recognised a boy after God's own heart, and I could not help being struck by the workings of grace, already manifest in one of such tender years.

After some minutes conversation, and before I could turn aside to speak to his father, he said to me: "Well, what do you think of the matter; will you take me to Turin to study?" I replied that I thought there was very good material to work upon. "And what do you think you can make of it?" Seeing that he fully grasped my meaning I said: "Something beautiful and acceptable to God." To this he replied:

"Then I must be the material and you are to fashion it; take me with you therefore." "But," I said, "I am afraid that your delicate health would not stand the strain of much study." "I don't think we need fear on that point," he said. "God's given me health and every assistance till now, and He will surely help me in the future." I then asked him what he thought of doing when his preliminary course was finished. To this he replied: "If I could hope for such a favour from God, I ardently desire to become a priest." "Very well," I replied; "now I want to see whether you are able to learn quickly; take this little book and study this page of it; tomorrow I shall see if you know it.

I then sent him to see the other boys and to join in their games, while I talked to his father. But a little surprise awaited me, for hardly ten minutes had elapsed when Dominic came back, and said with his usual pleasant manner: "If you like I will recite that page to you now." I took the book in some astonishment, and this only increased when he recited the page by heart, and could explain any passage in it. "Well done," I said, "as you have anticipated your lesson, I shall anticipate my answer. I will take you to Turin and you will be one of my chosen boys; you must pray that God will help both you and me to do His Holy Will."

Not knowing how to express his great gratitude he took my hand, and said: "I hope my behaviour will never give you cause for complaint."

Chapter VII

Dominic Comes to the Oratory of St. Francis of Sales. His Manner of Life.

Nothing is more characteristic of youth than its tendency to changeableness. A decision is taken on a certain thing today, tomorrow all will be changed; there may be virtue in a heroic degree one day, but on the next the opposite may manifest itself; and this is where there is need of guidance and firmness in education, lest unhappy results should follow. There was no sign whatever of this in Dominic. All the virtues seemed to grow together in him and he was able to practice them all in combination.

Directly he came to the Oratory, he came to my room, in order to place himself, as he said, entirely in the hands of his Director. He at once caught sight of an inscription which bore the favourite words of .St. Francis of Sales: "Da mihi animas, caetera tolle." He began to read it attentively, and I desired him to grasp the meaning. So I helped him to make it out, the translation being: "Give me souls; take away everything else!" "He seemed to reflect a moment, and then he said: "I think I understand; here the aim is not to gain money, but to win souls, and I hope that my soul will be included in the number."

His mode of life was just the routine life of school work; and at first there was nothing extraordinary to remark, beyond his scrupulous observance of every rule. At study or any other duty, he was at once diligent and zealous. Convinced that the Word of God is the guide to Heaven, he was particularly attentive to instructions and sermons, and from them he gathered maxims and rules of conduct which formed his constant guide.

He always made a point of asking for explanations of difficulties, and thus he was able to make continual progress in virtue, and in exactness in the performance of his duties, so that it would be difficult to go beyond the excellence he attained. He had already requested the favour of having his faults pointed out, so that his conduct towards all became equally praiseworthy; he was very apt at noticing what should be avoided in the conduct of a companion, and what should be imitated, and Dominic chose his companions accordingly.

The year 1854 was drawing rapidly to its close. It was a memorable year throughout the Catholic World, for all were awaiting the declaration of the Dogma of the Immaculate Conception. We, at the Oratory, were preparing to celebrate the occasion with due solemnity, and endeavouring to draw some spiritual advantage from it.

Savio was one of those who felt a desire to celebrate the great day in the manner most acceptable to Our Lady. He wrote out on nine pieces of paper an act of virtue to be practised every day of the Novena, drawing out one each day. These he faithfully put into practice, and approached the Sacraments with great devotion. On the evening of December 8th, Dominic knelt before the Altar of Our Lady, and, with the approval of his Confessor, renewed the promises made at his First Communion, begging particularly that he might be faithful to the last of the four, repeating his petition several times. Strengthened thus in fervour by his recourse to the Immaculate Mother of God, his conduct appeared so edifying, and included such acts of virtue, that I began to note them down so as not to let them be forgotten.

Coming now to describe the particular doings of the boy I find that I am confronted with quite an array of events and virtuous actions deserving of mention. For the sake of greater clearness I propose to group together certain incidents which deal with one phase or one particular matter, rather than to adhere to a strict chronological sequence.

Chapter VIII

His Studies at the Oratory. His Conduct at School. His Dealings with Quarrels and Special Dangers.

Having already laid a good foundation at Mondonio for the study of Latin, and owing to his powers of application and exceptional talent, Dominic was soon raised to the fourth class, which, according to present scholastic arrangements, would correspond to the second course of Latin grammar. During this course he was one of the pupils of Professor Bonzanino, for at that time classes for students were not yet conducted at the Oratory itself. Were I to speak here of his conduct, of the advancement he made, of his exemplary behaviour, I should have to repeat what his previous masters said of him. I shall therefore restrict myself to relating some incidents which were noted down during this period by those who were closely associated with him. The Professor himself often said that he could not recollect ever having had a pupil more attentive, more respectful than young Savio, for he was quite a model in everything. There was never any affectation about his manner or appearance; he was always careful and courteous, so that his companions, many of whom were drawn from good families, were anxious to become friendly and to converse with him. If the professor noticed a pupil who was restless and troublesome, he contrived to put him near Dominic, who, in his own tactful way, was sure to get him to keep silence, and apply himself to study or the work then in hand.

It is during this year that the record of Dominic's life gives us an incident full of heroism, and which is the more remarkable when his youth is taken into consideration, for he was only fourteen when he came to the Oratory. The occurrence in question concerns two of his school fellows, between whom a fierce quarrel had arisen, on account of some remarks on a point of family honour. The quarrel proceeded from the exchanging of insults to the giving of blows and stone throwing. Dominic came to hear of this quarrel, but he saw the difficulty of trying to interfere, for both boys were older and bigger than he was. However he found means for approaching each in turn, urged them to give up their hatred, and pointed out that anger and revenge were against the commandments of God; he wrote to each of them, threatening to acquaint their parents and their master, but the headstrong boys were not to be influenced; their minds had become so embittered that all entreaties were in vain. Apart from the risk of bodily injury to themselves, Dominic was most concerned with the offence against God, and he was eager to find some means of effectually interfering, but was perplexed as to the manner of doing so.

He then seemed to have an inspiration. He waited for the boys after school, and contriving to speak to each alone, he said: "Since you will persist in this insane and sinful quarrel I ask you to accept one condition." Each agreed, provided it did not interfere with their challenge of a fight with stones, and indulged in some very unbecoming language in reference to his enemy. The very language was enough to make Savio shudder, but desirous of preventing a greater evil he said: "The condition I wish to impose does not interfere with the challenge: "Then what is it?" "I shall not tell you till you meet for the duel."

They thought he was making game of them, but Savio insisted that he was quite serious and that he would be on the scene. Neither could conjecture what his plan was.

The place for the fight was a lonely spot outside the town. The boys, getting more and more incensed, were almost going to fight on the way, but Dominic managed to prevent them. The scene of action was reached, and the boys took up their positions at a little distance from each other, and had by them the stones they were to hurl. Now was Dominic's time for mediation. He stepped in the middle and said: "Before you commence to fight you must fulfil the condition you agreed upon." So saying he drew out of his coat pocket a crucifix and held it up in the air. "I desire," he said, "that each of you should look on this crucifix, and then if you will throw, you must throw the stone at me and say: "Our Saviour died pardoning his very persecutioners; I, a sinner, am about to offend Him by an act of open revenge."

Having said this, he threw himself on his knees before the one who seemed most enraged, and said: "Throw your stone at me; let me have the first blow." A shiver seemed to go through the boy thus addressed. "No," he exclaimed, "I couldn't do it. I am not so mean as that. I have nothing against you."

On hearing this Dominic turned to the other boy, who had been watching in amazement, and made the same proposal to him. He too refused such a cowardly act.

Then Dominic got up and said, with great earnestness: "You are both ashamed to commit this act of brutality against me; and yet you would commit it against God and lose your soul by grievous sin." And he held up the crucifix again.

This proved too much for the two boys; they were moved by his true Christian charity and his courage. One of them confessed that he felt a cold shiver, and felt thoroughly ashamed that he had forced a friend of Savio's character to take such extreme measures. Wishing to make him some amends, he forgave entirely the boy with whom he had quarrelled and promised to go to Confession at once. Thus Dominic secured a victory for charity and taught the boys a lesson. Is it too striking an act of courage to recommend for example to young school boys? This incident would have remained a profound secret, had it not been related by both boys who were the partners to the challenge.

It will be gathered from this incident that Dominic had gained great influence over his companions, but he often had to put up with annoyance from some who tried to draw him into undesirable practices. On one occasion in fact he had almost consented to go off with some boys, who wished him to join them at play instead of going to school, but the arguments against it arose so vividly before him, that he not only rejected the proposal for himself, but convinced the others that it would be wrong, and made them go with him to school.

At the end of that year he was among the very best of those who were promoted to a higher class, but when his next year began there were already signs that his health would need careful attention, and it was thought more prudent to let him have some private teaching at the Oratory, where intervals of rest and fewer tasks could be given him. Under this arrangement his health seemed to improve a good deal, so that he was again sent out to the higher classes in the town, this time to Professor Picco, who was held in the highest estimation as a teacher.

Several interesting facts are recorded of this year of rhetoric, and they will be related in their turn as the narrative proceeds.

Chapter IX

Dominic Forms the Resolution of Striving After Perfection.

In the above chapters we have considered Dominic as a student going through his scholastic course, and have insisted principally on his talents and industry. His spiritual advancement was of even greater importance in his eyes. Savio had been at the Oratory for six months when he heard a sermon delivered there on an easy method of arriving at the perfection of the saints. The preacher brought out particularly these three points that impressed themselves deeply on Savio's mind: first, that it was God's will that we should become perfect; secondly, that it was easy to become so; thirdly, that an exceeding great reward is laid up for those who arrive at perfection. The effect of the sermon on Dominic was to set his heart aglow with love of God. For some days he was extraordinarily quiet, so that his companions began to remark it, and I noticed it myself. I began to think that his health was commencing to give way again, so I questioned him about it.

His answer was put very quaintly: "If I am suffering at all," he said, "it is from something beneficial." I asked him to explain: he replied that he had been thinking over the sermon and was seized with the desire of becoming a saint; that it now appeared to him much easier than he had thought, and asked for some special guidance in regard to his behaviour. I very naturally praised his good intentions, but pointed out that it would not be beneficial for him to be disturbed and uneasy about it, for in such disquiet of soul the voice of God could not be heard. I told him he should be always happy and cheerful, to be exact in the practices of piety and his other duties, and to take his recreation regularly with his companions.

One day I told him I wished to make him a little present, but that I left the choice of it to him. "I do not desire anything else," he replied, "but to become perfect; if I do not obtain that I shall be fit for nothing." On another occasion we were discussing the etymology of names, and he put the question: "What does Dominic mean?" Some one answered: "Belonging to God:" "See then," he promptly replied, "if I was not right in saying that I ought to become a saint; even my very name says that I belong to God; therefore it shall be my constant endeavour to become a saint."

These and similar words on other occasions may seem extraordinary in so young a boy, but Dominic meant them in all seriousness; and his use of them, just referred to, was not because he was not leading a holy life; on the contrary; but it was because he wished to undertake penances, and remain for hours in prayer, things which his superiors decided were not suitable for his years or health, or his occupations.

Chapter X

Zeal for the Salvation of Souls.

The chief recommendation given to Dominic, to help him to attain perfection, was to endeavour to gain souls to God, for no action is more meritorious than to co-operate in the salvation of souls, for which Our Divine Saviour shed His Precious Blood. Dominic had a particular intuition of the importance of this good work, and on several occasions he said: "If I could help to gain my companions to God, what a happiness it would be!" It was on this principle that he never let any occasion go by of doing something to this end, and accordingly he frequently gave friendly advice or warning to those of the boys whose conduct was not approved of.

He had a particular horror of anything in the nature of blasphemy or taking the name of God in vain; in fact, it worked upon him to such a degree that his health was quite affected by it. If he heard any words of that nature, as he passed along the streets, he would look down as though in sorrow, and make some pious ejaculation. A companion had often noticed him raise his cap and utter a few words of prayer when these blasphemies had been uttered. On another occasion, as he returned from school to the Oratory, he heard an elderly man utter some very blasphemous words. Dominic shuddered, and immediately offered up his pious ejaculation is reparation. But he was satisfied neither, nor disposed to let it pass. Summoning all his courage, and not at all affected by human respect, he went up to the man and asked him to direct him to the Oratory. The boy's gentle manner immediately softened the man's anger, and he replied, very affably: "No, I am sorry, I don't know where it is." "Then there is another favour you can do me," said Dominic. "Oh, what is it?" The boy then came nearer and said in a low voice, only audible to the man in question: "It would be a great pleasure to me, if, when you are angry again, you would use words that are not blasphemous."

The man was naturally astonished at such a request from a boy, but there was something of admiration in his suprise; he replied: "Well done, you are right, it is a very bad habit, that I am determined to overcome."

But Dominic's manner with young offenders was different. He once heard two little boys quarrelling at their games outside the house, and one of them in his boyish anger used the Holy Name. Dominic was pained, as he always was when this occurred, so he stepped between the two boys and made them patch up their quarrel. Then he turned to the one that he had heard utter the name of God and said to him: "Come with me, there is something to be done, with which you will be pleased." He took him off to a church, near by, and both went up to the altar. There he made the boy kneel down and ask pardon for his profane use of the Holy Name. The boy did not know the act of contrition, so Dominic made him say it after him, and added to it some pious ejaculations, to atone for the irreverence offered to God.

Pursuing the same plan, Dominic made himself acquainted chiefly with the lives of those Saints who had spent their lives in the salvation of souls. A favourite topic with him was the missionary life, and what missionaries were actually undertaking at that time; and as it was impossible for him to help them materially, he offered daily prayers for their welfare, and at least one Communion a week. Strangely enough I have often heard him exclaim: "How many souls there are in England awaiting our assistance; there is nothing would please me more, had I the strength and virtue, than to go there and help, by preaching and good works, to gain them to Jesus Christ." He frequently lamented the lack of zeal in this direction, and also as regards the proper instruction of children in the truths of the Faith. It was his idea, that as soon as he was a cleric, he would go back to Mondonio, gather the children together, and teach them their catechism and to lead good lives. And he gave practical proof of this, for he often taught catechism in the church of the Oratory, and if any boy was backward, or had been neglected in regard to his religion, Dominic was always glad to take him in hand to instruct him, and prepare him for the Sacraments.

This of course could not be carried on without remarks from those who thought his zeal was out of place, and that such things should only be mentioned in church. A companion rebuked him once for talking on the life of some Saint in recreation time, and asked him why he did so. Dominic's answer was so full of genuine zeal for the good of souls, which, he remarked, had been redeemed with a great price, that it made a deep impression on those around.

During the intervals he spent at home for the holidays, Dominic put this zeal of his into practical effect; for he would gather other boys around him?and he had quite a gift for attracting them?and by conversations and stories he gave them good instruction and counsel, He also took home several objects of piety from the Oratory, and distributed them judiciously by way of rewards among these companions. It was therefore quite customary for several to accompany him to Mass and the Sacraments, and this good work had a lasting effect. During these holidays he was brought into contact with many people of all ages and conditions, for Dominic's manner had an attraction for all; and to all of them, in one way or another, he was the means of some spiritual advantage. No wonder that his reputation began to spread, even at that time. Dominic's guiding motto was, that no occasion for doing good to souls, or of offering some little act of reparation to God, should be missed; and this accounts for his constant zeal, and his visits to the Blessed Sacrament, in which he generally managed to be accompanied by a friend or some one he wished to bring to a better life.

Chapter XI

Various Incidents. His Attractive Manner with His Companions.

Although Dominic, as we have seen, was imbued with the desire to do good to souls, it did not, as some mistaken people might imagine, tend to make him melancholy or mournful. On the contrary, he was the life of the recreation time, though he very wisely knew how to turn every opportunity to account. When others had something to say or a story to tell, he never interrupted or criticised; but when conversation flagged, he had an inexhaustible fund of entertaining information and anecdotes which were highly interesting to his companies. He knew just when to seize the opportunity of speaking, if it were necessary to deal with grumbling or murmuring, or something not approved of.

His manner was so cheerful and attractive that he counted among his companions even those who were least disposed to piety, or were of an opposite nature to his own, and they always took in good part whatever insinuation or hint he might give them.

Once when the boys were at play in an open space, a man came up and joined in the conversation. He was amusing at first, and had a story or two that suited the curiosity of young people. But when he had made himself at home a little; he went on to speak of religious subjects and priests and the like, and treated them with ridicule and disrespect. Many of the boys noticed the change in his conversation and went off to play; others stayed on. But then Dominic arrived. He stopped for a moment to listen, but immediately saw what the man was about, and without any hesitation said to the boys round him: "Don't stay here listening to such a degraded man; he is only trying to corrupt souls." The boys were accustomed to Dominic's influence in regard to such things, and all moved away, leaving the man alone. The latter retired discomfited, and never tried his persuasive arts in that neighbourhood again.

This influence of Dominic's gradually increased, so that he could usually persuade the boys against any course in which he saw that evil might lurk. There was at the Oratory, at the time, a little society composed of the better and more able boys, who endeavoured to check any wrongdoing amongst the rest, and to deal with any unruly ones amongst them. Savio belonged to it and played a foremost part in it. Whatever little presents came to him he reserved them to add weight to his persuasion. Sometimes he would seize an opportunity in the games, when a boy on whom he had designs was a partner of his, to ask him to promise to go to Confession with him on the following Saturday. As Saturday usually seemed a long way off, the boy generally consented; but Dominic did not let him forget it, and when Saturday came he would take the boy off to church, as pleased with the success of his little ruse as a sportsman is in securing his prize. In this way it often happened that a boy, on whom a hundred sermons would be lost, would at once succumb to some novel method invented by Dominic's zeal for souls.

However, it occasionally happened, that on the appointed day, the boy who had promised to accompany him to Confession, would be missing. As soon as Dominic saw him again he would say: "Ah, you disappointed me; you didn't keep your promise." The boy would bring forward some excuse, but he was never able to convince Dominic, who easily explained to the boy that he had been caught in one of the devil's tricks for putting off Confession. He would then go on to show him how happy he would be afterwards if he made a good Confession, and get him to make another promise. It always happened that these boys would go to Dominic afterwards and tell him how glad they were for having followed his advice, and that they would go frequently to the Sacraments in future.

It is a common thing, that among a great number of boys, a few are left more or less severely alone, whether on account of their peculiar character, or of some defect, or something uninviting about them; sometimes, too, these are the object of the ridicule and torment of their companions, and are sorely in need of a friend. Dominic was always on the look out for these. He was frequently in their company, entertaining them in one way or another. Others, who through ignorance or neglect, were disposed to be mischevious or bad, Dominic took in hand, and always brought them to a better frame of mind. With the sick again he was in great demand; so that in one way or another

Savio was a real apostle and put into practice his great ideal of drawing souls to God.

Chapter XII

His Spirit of Prayer. His Devotion to the Holy Mother of God. The Month of May.

Dominic was evidently endowed with special gifts from God, and among them was his assiduity and fervour in prayer. It seemed to be part of his very nature to converse with God, and no matter where he was, or what noises or games might be going on around him, his recollection was never disturbed, and his ejaculations were none the less frequent. At the general prayers of the boys, his manner can only be described as that of an angel; his attitude was devotion itself; he never seemed to want to rest even his elbows, but, kneeling, and with hands joined, his eyes cast down, he gave himself up to communing with God. To look at him thus was to be edified.

In 1854 the Count Cays was elected President of the Sodality of St. Aloysius, that was established at the Oratory. The first time he was present at the functions of the Sodality, he saw a boy at prayer with such an air of rapt devotion, that he was immediately struck by him. He inquired about him afterwards, and of course, it was our young friend. Dominic always managed to spend some part of his recreation in the chapel, generally getting a companion to go in with him, though he need not stay as long as Dominic did.

His devotion to Our Blessed Lady was like a burning fire within him. Every day he practised some act of mortification in her honour. Attracted by her heavenly beauty he had no desire of gazing on things of earthly mould, and the thought of her purity and modesty prevented him from taking interest in the ordinary entertaining sights of the town which so much attract the average boy. This abstraction or deep recollection, when out in the streets, was frequently remarked upon by his companions, and he generally explained it by saying that he was thinking of something far more interesting in connection with Our Lady and Heaven. To her he offered special devotions in the course of the day, particularly on Friday, in honour of the seven dolours, and he placed his own purity of soul in the keeping of that immaculate Virgin.

It was therefore a natural development that he should be carried away with special fervour during the month of May. There were always extra services in the church for the benefit of the public, and the boys took part in them. But Dominic was not satisfied with that. He arranged with certain companions to perform extra devotions every day, and he prepared a stock of examples and anecdotes concerning the devotion to Our Lady; with the aid of these he urged not a few boys to make an effort to celebrate the month with fervour. Needless to say, he received Holy Communion every day during that period and was a shining example to all those that came in contact with him.

A little incident is told in connection with this month. It was proposed by someone that a little altar should be erected in the dormitory to which Dominic belonged, and a collection was made all round for contributions towards its expense. Savio found himself among the number of boys who had no pocket money at the time; yet it was not to be thought of that he should be out of the contribution to so good a cause. He soon conceived a plan. He had among his books one that was of some value, which he had received as a prize. He proposed that this should be sold and the proceeds given to the altar. Others thought they would adopt the same plan; they accordingly got together a few of their things that might be desirable in the eyes of companions, and arranged to have a sort of lottery. Purchasers were soon found, and the result was ample for the decoration of the altar. Its adornment was to be done after night-prayers, by special permission, but Dominic was expressly advised to go to bed, as he had not been well of late; he obeyed, but it was quite a sacrifice for him to be deprived of doing something that he thought tended directly to the honour of her, of whom he was one of the most devout clients.

Chapter XIII

His Frequentation and Devout Reception of the Sacraments.

The confirmed experience of those who have assisted in the spiritual training or the general education of the young is, that the Sacraments of Confession and Holy Communion are the best safeguards and the strongest supports for that critical period of their life. If you can show me a boy who frequently receives the Holy Sacraments, it will be enough to convince me that he will pass through the years of youth, reach the age of manhood and maturity, and, if God so disposes, arrive at a venerable old age, and all during that time will be an example to those who know him. This should be impressed upon the young so that they may form this excellent habit: it should be seriously considered and grasped by all who share in the education of the young, so that they may assist them to put it into practice.

Apart from certain establishments, few in number, it was not usual in the time we are treating of, for children or adults to go frequently to the Sacraments, and so Dominic Savio had only been accustomed to go once a month to Confession and Communion before he came to the Oratory. But from that time he began to go more often. In fact it had been stated in the pulpit of the Oratory Chapel, that if the boys were really desirous of walking in the path of virtue, and persevering in it, they should practise three things: to go regularly to the Sacrament of Penance; to approach the Holy Table very frequently; to open their heart freely to their confessor. Dominic had noted down these counsels, for in such things he had a special knowledge of what was important.

He chose his confessor, and only had the one during his stay at the Oratory. In order to make quite sure that everything was correct, and to form a right estimation of his conscience, he made a general confession. Then he began to go every fortnight, and then weekly. His habit of monthly Communion was soon altered to a weekly one, and then to several times a week, and then to a daily one. At one time he seemed to become scrupulous and wished to confess oftener, but his confessor forbade him to go more than once a week, and he adhered to this direction.

But in this confessor he had the utmost confidence, and opened his whole soul to him. Even out of confession he often consulted him about the affairs of his soul, and in regard to a change of confessor he very acutely said: "The confessor is the soul's physician. You do not change your doctor unless he proves unworthy of your confidence, or unable to deal with your complaint. Neither of these cases applies to me. I have entire confidence in my confessor, and I do not know of any diseases of the soul that he cannot cure." However, this confessor directed him to go to another priest from time to time, especially at the monthly exercises for a good death; and the boy did so.

In these matters, indeed, he had special gifts. He used to say that he could not possibly be in need of spiritual comfort or strength;for he got all the guidance he required from his confessor, and all the desires of his soul were satisfied in the delights of Holy Communion; nothing could be added to his happiness, until it was time for him to be admitted to the unveiled presence of Our Lord, whom he now beheld on the Altar with the eyes of Faith.

It was this frame of mind that conduced to Dominic's perpetual calm and cheerfulness, and the special joy that seemed to accompany his daily life. However, it must not be imagined for a moment that he was not observant in the extreme, lest anything should prevent his being prepared to go daily to the Holy Sacrament; on the contrary, his conduct was on all occasions singularly without blemish. I have questioned those who were with him during his three years amongst us, and who lived the same student's life with him, and not one of them could, after due reflection, bring forward any defect or negligence, or suggest any virtue in which he was lacking; and yet boys have a high standard when judging of such things in their companions.

In regard to his actual reception of Holy Communion, he used to say a special prayer of preparation the night before. In the morning he prepared with the other boys during Mass, and with his own particular devotion; but his thanksgiving cannot be said to have ever terminated.

It was quite an ordinary occurrence, that, if not specially called or aroused, he would not remember breakfast time or even school time, remaining in prayer, or rather in a sort of contemplation and adoration of the goodness of Our Divine Lord, who communicates with souls in His own ineffable manner.

If he could spend an hour during the day in the presence of the Blessed Sacrament, it was his utmost delight; but he always found time for a visit every day, and got someone to go with him if possible. His favourite prayers were a series of acts in reparation to the Sacred Heart of Jesus; they were a well known devotional practice, and to be found in most prayerbooks; in order that his communions might be more fruitful and meritorious, and that there might be a motive of renewed fervour every day, he always had a definite intention in view. His intentions were thus distributed over the week:

SUNDAY. - In honour of the Blessed Trinity.
MONDAY. - For the welfare of spiritual and temporal benefactors.
TUESDAY. - In honour of my Patron Saint, Saint Dominic, and of my Guardian Angel.
WEDNESDAY. - In honour of Our Lady's Seven Dolours, for the conversion of sinners.
THURSDAY. - For the Souls in Purgatory.
FRIDAY. - In honour of the Sacred Passion of Christ.
SATURDAY. - In honour of Our Lady, to obtain her protection in life and death.

Whatever devotions were practised in honour of the Blessed Sacrament, he took part in them with eager joy and delight; and would accompany the priest when taking Holy Viaticum, if he were allowed. One day a priest was passing across a muddy street with the Blessed Sacrament, when Dominic was near. There had been a great deal of rain and it was muddy all round. But the boy took no head of that. He knelt in the mud and made his act of adoration. A companion remonstrated that he need not have knelt in the mud: that God did not command it, and did not wish him to dirty his clothes in that way. But that was not at all Dominic's view of such things; he replied that trousers as well as knees belonged to God; and should therefore be employed in His honour. "Whenever I approach the Sacramental Presence," he said, "I would not only throw myself in the mud, but even into a fiery furnace, for thus I should be consumed with that fire of infinite charity, which moved Our Lord to institute the Most Holy Sacrament.

On another occasion he noticed that a soldier was standing while the Blessed Sacrament was being carried by; Dominic did not like to invite the soldier to kneel down, so he took out his handkerchief, spread it on the ground, and made a sign that he might kneel on it. The soldier was a little confused at this hidden rebuke, but he left the handkerchief alone and knelt down where he was, in the middle of the street.

One of Dominic's delights was to be dressed as a cleric for the great Procession of the Blessed Sacrament on the Feast of Corpus Christi. His whole bearing revealed the depth of his Faith and the excess of his love.

Chapter XIV

His Mortifications.

IT will be rightly conjectured that many reasons forbade that Dominic should undertake any extraordinary penance: there was his age (he was only fourteen or fifteen); there was his delicate health; there was the innocence of his life. But he knew that it is difficult to maintain fervour and purity of soul without some austerity, and this consideration made him ready for penances and mortification; and by mortifications I do not here allude to the insults and unpleasantness that he had to bear, or to his continual restraint over his senses, whether in class, study or recreation. This form of penance was a habit with him.

I refer now to actual penances, painful to the body. In his fervour, and his devotion to the Mother of God, he had resolved to fast on bread and water every Saturday; but his confessor forbade it; he wished to fast during Lent; but after a week it came to the knowledge of the Director of the House, and that too was forbidden. He wished at least to do without breakfast, but consideration for his health made it prudent to forbid that also. What then was he to do to satisfy his desire for some bodily mortifications. As he was forbidden to do anything that affected his food, he began to afflict his body in other ways. He put some some sharp things into his bed, so that he might not be able to repose in comfort: he wanted a kind of hair shirt; but all these things were soon prohibited. He thought of something else. During the autumn and winter he managed to escape having extra blankets for his bed, so that during the cold of January he had only the summer coverings on his bed. This was discovered, because, one morning he was unwell, and had to remain in bed; and when the Director came to see him, he saw at once that he had insufficient covering for that severe weather. "Why did you do this?" the Director asked, "did you want to die of cold?"

"Oh, I shall not die of cold," he answered. "When in the stable at Bethlehem, or hanging on the Cross, Our Lord had less to cover Him than I have now." He was then forbidden to undertake any penance at all without express permission; and this command, though difficult, was obeyed.

Later on I saw that he was in some difficulty. He said he could not reconcile the command of the Gospel to do penance, with the prohibition he had received. "The penance God wishes from you," I said, "is simply obedience. If you obey, that will suffice for everything."

"Can you not allow me to do some other penance?"

"The only penance you are to do, is to bear patiently all that God sends you in this life."

"But those things must be put up with by necessity."

"Very well," I replied, "whatever you have to suffer by necessity, offer it to God, and it will become a virtue, and meritorious in the sight of God."

This counsel comforted his misgivings and he was never disturbed in that way again.

Chapter XV

The Mortification of His External Senses.

Any casual observer of Dominic's outward behaviour would have thought his composure so natural, that it must have been part of his character from birth; but those who were intimately associated with him, and had the care of his education, know very well that it was only gained by long and serious effort, assisted by the grace of God.

To obtain the guard he had over his eyes, he had to make so great and constant an effort, that he once told a friend that his head often ached in consequence of it; but the restraint he had acquired was so complete that no one ever saw him give an unguarded glance, or indulge his sight to the least degree. The eyes are like two windows, he would say, and it depends upon yourself whether you admit an angel or a devil by them.

One day a boy had brought in, doubtless unthinkingly, a paper with some unbecoming pictures in it. A group of boys gathered round to see them, and Dominic thought some sacred pictures were being shown. So he came up to look also; but as soon as he perceived of what nature the pictures were, he was surprised, and taking hold of the paper he tore it into pieces. The boys stood around in silence; then he quietly said: "Our eyes were given to see the beautiful things God has created, and you use them to gaze on such unseemly pictures, provided by the malice of satan for the ruin of souls. Perhaps you have forgotten what you have so often heard, that one evil glance may stain the soul with sin; and yet you indulge your eyes with such objects as that."

Some began to make excuses, but he easily showed them that they were but the snares of the devil, who could draw them on to sin by these means; and in the end no reply could be made to his arguments and recommendations.

To this care of the eyes he joined particular reserve in conversation. He never interrupted anyone who might be speaking, and he often broke off his own sentences in the middle, if another showed that he had something to say. His masters and associates all agree that he was never observed to have said a single idle word, whether in class or in study, or during the fulfilment of any duty. Even when he was the object of unkindness or insults, he had a careful reserve over his words.

One day he had spoken to a companion about a bad habit he had contracted. The latter forgot that this was a kindness, and answered with insults, and even struck and kicked him. Dominic was older and bigger than the other boy, and might easily have returned this treatment; but he sought no revenge but that of Christian charity: at first he became red in the face, but stifling all feeling of resentment he said: "I forgive you; you have done wrong; but do not try that sort of behaviour on others."

In regard to the mortification of all his senses, I shall restrict myself to a few incidents. In winter-time he had a novel way of treating his hands, for he was subject to chilblains, and these he exposed to the cold and wet as much as he could, so as to increase their size and painfulness; he even pricked them to make them smart the more. He thought that he was thus imitating, in a small degree, the wounds inflicted on the person of our Divine Lord. His companions assert that in the very cold weather he went along slowly to school, so as to be exposed to the weather as much as possible.

Wherever there are a number of young people living together, there are sure to be some who are ready with complaints. The arrangements of the house, the discipline, the bed time, and such things, all form the subject of complaint from different persons, and occasionally great disturbances are caused. Savio was quite the opposite of this. He rejoiced if there were something that might be taken exception to, and, particularly in his diet, he was always satisfied and equally pleased.

He was economical to a degree, regarding the food as a gift of God, and therefore not to be despised, even in the smallest way. He was always ready to do a service to others, particularly to the sick, and he eagerly seized occasions for doing this, since his health made him unable to undertake anything of a tiring nature.

Little examples of his mortification, charity, self-forgetfulness, humility, and the like, might easily be multiplied, but these things were part of Dominic's very life, and went to make up that perfect whole which constitutes a pleasing offering in God's sight.

Chapter XVI

The Confraternity of the Immaculate Conception.

Something has been said above about Dominic's devotion to Our Blessed Lady, and it may be well imagined that the circumstances of December, 1854, provided occasions for extra fervour that were not lost upon him.

On the eighth of that month the Sovereign Pontiff defined the Dogma of Our Lady's Immaculate Conception, and the Catholic world was filled as with a wave of devotion. Young Savio was always practical in his manifestation of fervour. His idea was not only to celebrate the event, but to set on foot something that might be a permanent remembrance, and might be productive in years to come of a continual stream of devout clients of Our Lady.

He therefore set to work amongst his closest friends, and proposed to them the formation of a sodality or association, to be called the Sodality of the Immaculate Conception. Its object was to obtain the special protection of Our Lady during life and particularly at the hour of death. The means proposed were to practice and promote acts of devotion in honour of the Mother of God, and the adoption of the practice of frequent Communion by all members. It was to have a special rule and these were the subject of long consideration, so that they were only in their final shape by June 8th, 1856, about nine months before his death. These were read out by him before the Altar of Our Lady on that day. The articles were of an exhaustive character, twenty-one in number, providing for the regular meeting of the members, the spiritual duties undertaken, and the means for gaining the chief ends mentioned above. These rules were all submitted to the judgment of the Director, and concluded with an appeal to Our Blessed Lady to assist the associates and bless their efforts. Several of those who took part in the formation of this society were distinguished, like Dominic, for their piety and talents. One in particular was gifted with exceptional brilliance, and being afterwards ordained as a secular priest, he had a most fruitful apostolate, and took a large share in the arrangements for the opening of the Sanctuary of Our Lady, Help of

Christians, at Turin, during the octave of which celebrations he was called to his reward. While still a cleric he founded the Sodality of the Blessed Sacrament, which has since been a traditional sodality in our schools, and by its means effected great good among the boys of the Oratory.

Chapter XVII

Dominic's Intimate Associates.

FROM much of the foregoing it will be concluded that Dominic was a friend to all, and was regarded by all as a friend. If anyone did not feel drawn to him in a particular manner, it was impossible not to treat him with respectful regard. He was of such excellent dispositions, partly from his natural gifts, partly from his training and efforts, that he was often given charge of boys who needed some special care and skilful handling, so that he might gradually bring them up to the standard that flourished at the Oratory. In carrying out these charges he was particularly apt at profiting of every occasion that presented itself, whether in recreation, or walks, or church.

But if he was regarded as a friend by the boys in general, he was something more to those who were associated with him in the Sodality of the Immaculate Conception. These were his co-workers, counsellors, and intimate friends. They were brought together for their extra devotions, their talks and arrangements, their discussions concerning the boys who were entrusted to their care for special guidance, and all other items concerning the apostolate of those who belonged to the Sodality, and which was far reaching in its scope. These conferences and propositions were made with the approval of the Director, but were held by the boys themselves.

Savio was the prime mover in these meetings, and, in fact, was looked up to as the teacher and guiding spirit. There were, however, several prominent members, who were very like him in their zeal and piety, and in their skill and capabilities in assisting in the training of their younger companions. Many of these are still living, and engaged in the priesthood, or in prominent positions; it would therefore, perhaps, not be tactful to speak of them directly. But I have thought it useful to call attention to two of them who have already been called away to their eternal reward. They are Camillus Gavio, and John Massaglia. The former only remained at the Oratory two months, but it was long enough to leave a lasting remembrance.

His piety had always been conspicuous, and with this he possessed remarkable talents, particularly for painting and sculpture; so much so, that the municipality of Tortona, his native city, had awarded him a scholarship, so that he might come to the Schools of Turin, to continue his studies and artistic training.

Shortly before his arrival at the Oratory he had recovered from a serious illness. This doubtless accounted for much of his quiet, retiring life, for he was practically only then convalescent, and at a distance from his home and friends. Moreover, he knew none of the boys at the Oratory, and all these circumstances combined to make him rather a spectator of, than a partner in the games, and he was often noticed with a far away, abstracted look. Savio soon made his acquaintance and got into conversation. He had quickly elicited the main facts of the boy's life, including his late illness. But this last item should be described in the words of the actual speakers. The newcomer had described briefly his illness, which was concerned with a weakness of the heart, and had brought him to death's door.

"You desired very much to be cured, I suppose?" enquired Dominic.

"No, not a great deal; I only desired that the Will of God might be done."

No more than this was required to convince Savio that his new acquaintance was gifted with extraordinary piety, and he secretly rejoiced at this acquisition to the Oratory; he therefore followed up the boy's response by remarking: "Whoever desires to do the Will of God, is anxious for his own sanctification; do you ever feel this desire?"

"Oh yes, it has long been my chief ambition."

"Very good; the number of our friends increases daily; you will join our inner circle of those who have the same ambition as you have."

The new boy agreed, and a discussion was held as to his future conduct. Savio pointed out to him, that at the Oratory sanctity consisted principally in being happy; that the boys took every care to avoid sin, as the great enemy, to do all duties as well as possible, and to perform the practices of piety with exactitude. Servite Domine in laetitia is to be our motto.

This advice of Dominic's seemed to fall like a healing balm on the soul of Camillus. He became a close companion of Dominic's, and from him learnt the secrets of great holiness that he had himself acquired. With such a guide, and with his own excellent good will and dispositions, it was no wonder he made rapid progress in virtue, so as to become prominent even among those who were themselves all of a very high standard of exactitude and piety.

However, his rapid progress in piety was like his swift course towards heaven. The illness he had described to Dominic had left effects that could not be removed by medical aid, and it was soon evident that he was in a very dangerous condition. Every care from physicians and friends was his, but in vain. It was time for him to go to that Divine Lord whose Will he had so faithfully sought to do, and after receiving the Sacraments with great edification, he died on December 30th, 1856.

Dominic was his constant attendant during his illness, and would readily have watched by him all night, but he was not allowed. When he was told that his companion had died, he asked to go and see the body, and looking at the face of his friend he said with emotion: "Farewell, Gavio; I am quite sure that you have gone to Heaven; so prepare a place for me. However, I shall always be a friend to you, and shall pray for the repose of your soul as long as I am left here on earth."

The Sodality of the Immaculate Conception had special rules for the prayers and Communions to be offered for the deceased members, and Dominic immediately arranged for them to be carried out. His words and recommendations to his companions on this occasion were typical of that gravity, which he always displayed in regard to things of the spiritual life, of the importance of which he always had an intimate conviction.

Chapter XVIII

Dominic Savio and John Massiglia.

There was a boy at the Oratory whose character and career bore a striking similarity to Dominic's. He had come to Turin at the same time; he had come from a little place quite close to Mondonio, so that they were practically from the one district. He had the same intentions as Dominic, to embrace the ecclesiastical state, and he was inspired with a like eagerness to advance in the science of the saints. This was John Massiglia.

He had been talking one day to his friend about their future hopes, and after their exchange of ideas Dominic said: "It will not be sufficient for us merely to desire to become priests; there are means to be adopted to acquire the virtues that are suitable to that state." John replied that he was fully aware of it, but that he had confidence that they would have the grace to acquire them, if they were chosen to be among the ministers of Jesus Christ.

There had been some special sermons and exercises in preparation for the Easter Communions, and these two had taken part in them with singular devotion. After their Communion Dominic said to his companion: "I very much desire that we should be true friends; friends, that is, in regard to the affairs of the soul. I propose that from now we each admonish the other in regard to anything that may be thought useful for our spiritual advancement. If you see anything wrong in my conduct tell me immediately, that I may correct it; or if you think of any good I ought to perform, point it out to me."

His friend promised to do so, "though," he said, "there will be no opportunity, and on the condition that you do the same for me, who am in much greater need of such an arrangement." Dominic replied that that was not the time for compliments, but that henceforth they would help each other in the progress of their soul.

From that time, Dominic Savio and John Massiglia were intimate friends, and it was a true and perfect friendship, since it was founded upon real charity, and nourished by the frequent intercommunion of those pious suggestions and experiences which are prompted only by solid virtue.

At the end of the scholastic year, after the examinations, all the boys were allowed to go to their homes for the vacation, but some always preferred to remain at the Oratory, both for the advantages of extra study and to continue their exercises of piety, which could scarcely be carried on at home. Savio and Massiglia were among the number. But I knew that both were eagerly expected by their parents to spend the holidays at home, and that a change and rest were necessary after their year's work at their books. I therefore met them both together and said:

"Why do you not prefer to go home for a time?" No answer was at first forthcoming; both began to smile. "What is the meaning of that smile?" I enquired. Then Dominic replied, "We know that our parents would like us to go home, and in one way we are anxious to go; but as long as birds are in their cage, they are safe from the hawk; once out of it, there is risk of falling into the toils of the enemy of souls."

But in spite of their good intentions and their desires to stay, I insisted on their going home for a time. They obeyed, but only stayed away the minimum time that I had appointed.

If a detailed description were to be given of this friend, it would be very similar to the one being given of Dominic himself, for they had the same ideals, and were led in the same paths of virtue. Massiglia was of far more robust build than Dominic, and his health never gave anxiety; in fact he was most promising in every way; particularly in regard to his progress in his studies. He had finished his course of rhetoric and had received the clerical habit, for which he had so ardently longed. But he was destined to enjoy his happiness only for a few months. Some indisposition, slight though it appeared to be, caused us to insist on his studies being laid aside for a time, and as he did not appear to recover he was sent to his native place, by the advice of the doctors. While there he wrote to his friend the following letter:

"My dear Friend,

" When I left the Oratory, I thought I should be away only for a short time, so that I did not think it necessary to bring any books or school things with me. But now it appears that my recovery will take time, and in fact the issue of my illness is quite uncertain. The doctor says I am improving, but I think I am gradually getting worse: we shall see which of us is right. My chief regret is that I must be away from the Oratory and from you, and have had to give up most of the exercises of piety which we used to practise. My only consolation is in the recollection of the days when we went together to Holy Communion, and the preparation we used to make for them.

"However, although we are separated in body, we shall remain united in heart and spirit. I want to ask you to get from my desk some manuscripts and the Latin copy of the Imitation of Christ, which is beside them, and send both on to me. You may imagine how tired I am of doing nothing. The doctor will not hear of my studying at all. I have plenty of time for consideration, and often wonder whether I am to be cured, or to go back again to the Oratory, or whether this is destined to be my last illness. In any case I feel ready to submit with joy to the Holy Will of God.

"If you have any suggestion to make tell me of it. Do not forget to pray for me, and if we may not have the opportunity of enjoying our former friendship I trust we shall enjoy together one day a happy eternity.

"Remember me to all my friends, particularly to the Sodality of Our Lady Immaculate.

"Believe me,

"Your affectionate friend,
"JOHN MASSIGLIA."

Dominic at once carried out his friend's request, and enclosed the following letter:

"My dear Massiglia,

"Your letter was a source of consolation to me, and to all your friends, for it at least showed that you were alive, a fact which we were beginning to doubt, and did not know whether to sing the Gloria Patri or the De Profundis. The things you have asked for are being sent. I will only remark that though Thomas à Kempis is a good friend, he is dead and gone; you must search for him in his writings, and make his counsel living again by putting it into practice.

"I see that you are desirous for the opportunities we have here for the performance of the spiritual exercises. You are right. When I am away from the Oratory I feel the same need. I used to try to make up for it by visiting the Blessed Sacrament every day, and getting some companions to go with me if they would. Besides the Imitation I used to read the Hidden Treasure, by St. Leonard of Port Maurice. You could do the same perhaps, if you feel disposed.

"You say that you do not know whether you will return to the Oratory or not. Truth to tell, I also feel that my health is showing alarming symptoms, and I have a presentiment that I am advancing with rapid strides towards the end of my studies and of my life. We can at least pray for each other, that we may have the grace of a happy death. Whichever one of us goes to Heaven first must prepare a place for the other, and will be able to stretch out a helping hand to lead him to his heavenly home.

"May God keep us in His Grace, and help us to become saints, for we may not have long to live. All your friends are longing for your return to the Oratory and send their kind remembrances to you. For myself

"I remain,

"Your most affectionate friend,
"DOMINIC SAVIO."

This illness of young Massiglia, as we have said, appeared slight at first; more than once he seemed quite recovered; but again relapsed, until he was quite suddenly brought to the point of death.

Fr. Vafrè, who was his Director while at Mondonio, writes: "He had time to receive the last comforts of Religion, and did so with greatest edification; he died the death of the just man who leaves this world to go straight to his reward."

Savio was profoundly grieved at the death of his close friend, and although resigned to the Will of God, he mourned his loss for some time. It was almost the only occasion that I had seen his gentle face covered with the tears of sorrow. His one consolation was to pray for his friend's soul, and to get others to pray for him. More than once he said: "Massiglia has gone to join Gavio in heaven, when shall I go to join them in the bliss of Paradise?"

As long as Dominic lived, he had his friend often in mind, particularly at Mass and at the spiritual exercises; he never ceased to recommend to God the soul of that friend, who, he felt, had been of such assistance to him. In fact this loss had more serious results than one would think, for it seriously affected the already weakened frame of the friend and his health, which had never been robust.

Chapter XIX

Special Graces Granted to Dominic. Some Particular Incidents.

As far as the generality of boys is concerned, it would be considered quite extraordinary for them to maintain the high standard of conduct, and the continual endeavour after virtue that has been described above; that innocence of life and performance of good works, penances, and acts of special fervour. But these things made up the ordinary rule of Savio's life. Nothing short of extraordinary, again, were his wonderful faith, his constant hope, his ardent charity, and his perseverance till his last breath.

I now wish to describe certain facts that are really out of the common, and which may perhaps some day be the subject of criticism. It may be well to point out to the reader, that the facts to be related are very like others related in the Bible or in the Lives of the Saints; moreover I am relating what occurred under my own notice, and the incidents are given with scrupulous care; the conclusions to be drawn must be left for the discreet reader.

Very often when Dominic went into the church, principally on his Communion days, or when the Blessed Sacrament was exposed, he fell into what was clearly a sort of rapture or ecstasy; and thus he would remain for a very long time, if he were not called away to fulfil his ordinary tasks.

It happened one day that he was absent from breakfast, from class, from the mid-day meal, and no one knew where he was; he was not in the study, nor in the dormitory. The Director was informed, and he had a suspicion that he knew where to find him, namely in the church, as had happened before. He went to the church, and up into the choir near the sanctuary; there stood the boy like a statue; one foot was in front of the other, and one hand was on a book stand near by, while the other was on his breast. His face was turned towards the sanctuary and his gaze fixed on the tabernacle. His lips were not moving. The Director called him; no reply; he shook him gently; then he turned and said: "Oh, is the Mass over!" "See," said the priest, showing him his watch; "it is two o'clock." The boy said he was sorry for his transgression of the rule, and the Director sent him off to dinner, saying: "If anyone asks you where you have been, say that you have been carrying out an order of mine." This was in case any inquisitive boy should put inopportune questions to him.

Another day, after making my usual thanksgiving, I was going out of the sacristy, when I heard a voice in the choir, as if someone were disputing. I went in to see what was the matter, and found Savio there. He was talking, and waiting every now and again as though listening to the answer. Among other things he said, I distinctly caught the words: "Yes, oh my God, I have already said it, and I say so again: I love Thee and will love Thee till my last breath. If Thou knowest that I should ever offend Thee, let me die; yes, I would die rather than commit sin."

I sometimes asked him what happened when he stayed behind like that. He would answer in all simplicity: "I become distracted, and losing the thread of my prayers, I behold such beautiful and entrancing sights that hours seem to go in a moment."

One day he came to my room and said: "Come quickly, Father, come with me, there is a good work to be done."

"Where am I to go," I said. "Make haste, make haste," he said. I hesitated, but as he insisted, and past experience had shown me the importance of such invitations, I went down with him. He went first, I followed. Down one street, then another, then a third, all in silence; there was yet another turning, and at a certain door he stopped; there he went up the stairs to the third floor, rang the bell vigorously, and turning to me said: "It is here that you are wanted." Then he went away.

The door was opened and a woman appeared. "Oh, make haste," she said, "quick, or it will be too late. My husband has abandoned his faith; now he is at the point of death and wishes to die a Catholic."

I went over at once to the bedside, to the sick man, who was indeed very anxious to put the affairs of his soul in order. I did what I could for the man without loss of time, and his confession was just completed, when the parish priest who had been sent for, arrived. He just had time to administer Extreme Unction with one anointing, when the man breathed his last.

Afterwards I asked Dominic how he knew that there was a man ill at that house; he did not answer, but looked at me with an air of sadness, and I noticed that tears were beginning to come. I did not question him further.

Purity of life, love of God, and his longing for heavenly things had made Dominic almost habitually absorbed in God. At times, even during recreation, these visitations would occur to him. He would drop out of the game and walk away alone. Asked why he left his companions he would answer: "My usual distractions are assailing me; it seemed to me that Heaven opened and I have to leave my companions for fear that I should say something that would appear to them ridiculous."

On one occasion something was being said about the reward of the innocent souls. Dominic had given his opinion, and by the thought of such things he was quite carried away; he became motionless at first, then dropped into the arms of someone standing near. These ecatacies in fact came on in many different places, in the study, going to and from school, and even during class.

It was remarkable that he often spoke about the Sovereign Pontiff, and expressed the desire of being able to see him, as he had something of great importance to tell him. As he had repeated this on several occasions, I one day asked him what the important matter was. He replied: "If I could have an interview with the Pope, I would tell him, that in spite of the great tribulations which he has to endure at present he should never slacken in his particular solicitude for England: God is preparing a great triumph for Catholicism in that kingdom."

"Why, what grounds have you for that statement?"

"I will tell you, but do not mention it to others, for they might think it ridiculous. But if you go to Rome, tell Pius IX. for me. This is why I think so. One morning, during my thanksgiving after Communion, I had a repeated distraction, which was strange for me; I thought I saw a great stretch of country enveloped in a thick mist, and it was filled with a multitude of people. They were moving about, but like men, who, having missed their way, are not sure of their footing. Somebody near by said: 'This is England.' I was going to ask some questions about it when I saw His Holiness Pius IX. as I had seen him represented in pictures. He was majestically clad, and was carrying a shining torch with which he approached the multitude as if to enlighten their darkness. As he drew near, the light of the torch seemed to disperse the mist, and the people were left in broad daylight. 'This torch,' said my informant, 'is the Catholic religion which is to illuminate England.' "

When I was in Rome in 1858 I related this to the Holy Father, who was greatly interested and said: "What you have told me confirms me in my resolution to do all that is possible for England, which has long been the object of my special care. What you have related is, to put it at its lowest estimation, the counsel of a devout soul."

There are many other facts of a somewhat similar nature, but which are out of place in a small life like this. I have left them on record, so that, when, in the opinion of others, their publication is demanded, they maybe given to the world.

Chapter XX

Dominic's Ideas About Dying and His Preparation for a Happy Death.

The brief years of Dominic's innocent life, as above related, may well be considered as a continual preparation for death. But he regarded the Sodality of the Immaculate Conception, which he had practically founded, as a secure means for obtaining the assistance of the Blessed Virgin, at the point of death, which many thought to be a not very remote contingency in Dominic's case. I do not know exactly whether he had a revelation concerning the time or circumstances of his death, or merely a presentiment of it, but it is certain that he spoke of it a good time before it occurred, and with such clearness and circumstantial knowledge, that it could not have been described more exactly by one who had actually witnessed his death.

On account of the state of his health, every care was taken to moderate his studies and his exercises of piety; but as an effect of his natural delicate build, and the constant spiritual effort, his strength gradually gave way. He had no misgivings about this himself, and had often said: "I must hurry, or else night will overtake me on the way," which meant that he had only a short time left to him, and that he should use it well in the performance of good works.

It is the custom at the Oratory for the boys, to make the exercises for a good death every month. This consists chiefly in approaching the Sacraments of Confession and Holy Communion as though it were to be for the last time. Pius IX. had granted several indulgences to this pious exercise. Dominic always made this preparation for a good death with an exactitude that could not be excelled. Among the prayers said in public on this day are an Our Father and Hail Mary for the one amongst us who shall be the first to die. On one of the monthly exercise days Dominic playfully said: "Instead of saying 'for the first one amongst us who is to die,' it ought rather to be: 'for Dominic Savio, who will be the first one amongst us to die.' " And this he remarked on more than one occasion.

In 1856, just before the month of May began, he went to his Director to ask for some special guidance in order to keep the month with particular devotion. The Director told him it should be done by the most exact fulfilment of one's duties, by receiving Holy Communion daily, and performing some little act in honour of Our Lady every day. Dominic then wished to know what special grace he should ask for, and was told to ask that Our Lady might obtain for him an improvement in health, and the grace to become more pleasing in the sight of God. To this Dominic replied: "Yes, I shall ask the grace to become a saint, that she may help me in the last morgent of my life and that I may die a holy death."

In fact during that month he seemed to be living only outwardly amongst us and to be more than usually in communion with the world of angels; and his efforts to do something in honour of Our Lady every day were remarkably successful, so much so, that a companion was prompted to remark to him: "If you do so much this year, how will you be able to improve upon it next year?" Dominic replied: "You may leave that to me; I must do all that is possible this year, and if I am here next year, I will answer your question."

In order that his failing health might have every care I arranged for a medical consultation. Dominic was examined by these specialists, and all wondered at his bright cheerfulness of disposition, the acuteness of his intellect, and the prudence displayed in his replies. Dr. Vallauri, of distinguished memory, who was one of the most eminent consulting physicians, said: "What a priceless treasure you have in this boy!"

I asked him what was the cause of the boy's gradual decline, that could be noticed almost day by day. He said it was the delicacy of his constitution, his precocious knowledge, and the constant highly strung tension of his whole being; these were too great a strain on his vital powers.

"Is there any remedy that you can suggest?"

"The best remedy, as far as I can see, is to let him go to Paradise, for which he seems to be quite ready; but the only thing that can prolong his life is to make him put his studies entirely aside, and let him have some light occupation suitable to his strength."

Chapter XXI

Dominic's Interest in the Sick. He had to Leave the Oratory for Change of Air. His Parting Words.

Dominic's gradual decline was not so rapid or so marked as to cause him to be continually in bed; he sometimes went into the class room, or the study, or helped in some light domestic work, as the doctor had suggested; but his chief delight was to attend on his sick companions whenever there chanced to be any. But he seemed to derive such pleasure from it that he doubted whether it could be meritorious in the sight of God.

However, while he waited upon their needs he was particularly pleased to be able to assist them in some spiritual way, and was very skilful in his method of so doing. He remarked to one companion that the poor body could not last for ever, so that it had to become weak some time or other and gradually be consumed; but then the soul which had been set free would go to its everlasting home, and enjoy an eternal happiness. If the medicine were distasteful, he would remark to the sick boy that it was not nearly as bad as the gall and vinegar of our Divine Lord, and that it was ordained by God that these remedies should be provided for the body.

Dominic's own health had already made it evident that he would have to leave the Oratory and go home for his native air. He had a great repugnance to this, for it interrupted his practices of piety; and in fact I had sent him to his home just before this, but he only remained there a few days and then returned to the Oratory. I must own that our regret was mutual and I would have made every sacrifice to keep him amongst us; I regarded him with the affection that a father has towards the best beloved of his sons. But the recommendations of the doctors made it clear that it would be against all prudence to keep him longer at the Oratory, especially as he had been troubled with a severe and obstinate cough for some days.

Notice was accordingly sent to his father and the day for his departure was fixed for March 1st, 1857. In order to make a sacrifice of his will to God, Dominic submitted to this arrangement, for he would have much rather ended his days at the Oratory. Somebody suggested to him that it would not be for long, and that he would return quite well and be able to continue his studies. But Dominic was under no misapprehension; he replied that he was going away and he knew quite well that he would never return.

On the evening before his departure he stayed with me a long time, so much so that he had no wish to leave me. He had a great many questions to ask, concerning chiefly his own method of action as an invalid, which now he was, and how he might make that state meritorious. I told him that he should offer his illness and his life to God. He was anxious about his past faults and whether I thought he would be saved. I assured him that whatever he might have committed was forgiven, and that he need have no fear of being saved. In regard to temptations, I counselled him to reply to the tempter that he had already given his soul to Our Lord, who had redeemed it with His Precious Blood.

He had many further questions about dying and about Heaven, and he seemed like one who had his foot upon the threshold of Heaven and wanted to know beforehand what it was like.

The day for his departure happened to be the day for the exercises of a happy death, and these he made with the utmost fervour. In fact I have no words in which to describe the devotion with which he approached the Sacraments, though it made a deep impression on me. He regarded these exercises as his actual preparation for death, and thought that perhaps his end might come at any moment.

His few preparations for departure were soon made, though they were carried out with that scrupulous care which showed that he regarded them as the last acts he would do at the Oratory. He went to each of his companions to say goodbye, and to several he gave a little message of advice or encouragement or recommendation. To one boy he owed a few pence. He called to him and said: "Come let us put our accounts right, or else there may be trouble in settling accounts with God." To his associates in the Confraternity of the Immaculate

Conception he had some special advice to give, and encouraged them always to have the greatest confidence in Our Lady.

When he was going he turned to me and said: "Then you will not have my body with you, and I must needs take it to Mondonio? It would have been but a brief inconvenience and then all would be over . . . . But the Will of God be done. If you go to Rome do not forget the message I have given you concerning England; pray that I may have a happy death, and that we may see each other again in Heaven.

We had reached the door of the Oratory leading out to the street. He still had hold of my hand, but he turned to his companions and said: "Goodbye, my friends, pray for me, and may we meet again in Heaven where there are no more partings." Just as he was leaving he said to me: "I would like a present as a souvenir." I asked him what he would prefer to have, a book for example? "No, something better than that." I thought perhaps he wanted something for his journey and suggested it to him. He replied: "Yes, it is exactly that, something for the journey to eternity. You have spoken of a plenary indulgence from the Pope, for those who are dying; I should like to participate in that."

I said I would willingly insert his name amongst those who should enjoy that privilege which I had obtained especially from Rome.

Thus he left the Oratory where he had spent the last three years. They had been three happy years for the boy, three years of continual edification for his companions and even for his superiors; he had left it now to return no more.

His parting salutations, so unusual in a boy, had astonished all of us. We knew that he suffered a good deal from his illness, but as he was nearly always up and about, we were not accustomed to regard it as causing immediate anxiety. His cheerful disposition also went far to conceal his sufferings. Therefore, although we were inclined to take his parting words seriously, and were greatly grieved at them, we still had hopes that he would return and continue his studies. But the sequel proved otherwise. He was ready for Heaven; during the few years of his boyhood he had merited the reward of the just, and it seemed that God designed to take him to Himself in the spring time of his life, and before he should encounter those dangers which bring shipwreck often even to the purest souls.

Chapter XXII

The Progress of his Illness. He Receives the Last Sacraments. Edifying Incidents.

Dominic had left the Oratory on the 1st of March. The journey home in the carriage and the change of scene appeared to do him good, and therefore it was not thought necessary that he should remain in bed. But after a few days he seemed to become weaker, his appetite was poor, and his cough more noticeable, so that the doctor was consulted. His opinion was that the boy was a great deal worse than he appeared. He had him put to bed at once, and as he thought there was some inflamation he had recourse to blood letting.

This remedy usually had great terrors for the young. The doctor therefore advised Dominic to fix his attention on something else, and to have patience and courage. The boy smiled and said: "What is such a little wound compared to those made by the nails in the hands and feet of our Saviour?" Then with the greatest tranquillity of mind, in almost a playful mood, and without the least sign of apprehension, he watched the whole operation. When it had been repeated several times he seemed to be somewhat better; the doctor thought there was a turn towards improvement; his parents thought likewise; but Dominic was not to be brought to their opinion. Guided by the thought that it is better to receive the Sacraments in good time, than to delay till it was too late, he sent for his father and said: "Father, I think it would be better to consult the heavenly physician. I wish to go to Confession and Communion."

His parents quite thought that he was on the road to recovery; it was with sorrow they heard such remarks as these, and it was just to satisfy his desire that they sent for the priest. He came at once, heard the boy's confession and, in accordance with his request, brought the Holy Viaticum.

The devotion and eager fervour displayed by Dominic under these circumstances is better imagined than described. Whenever he approached the Sacraments it was in the attitude and dispositions of a

Saint Aloysius, and now that he received them for what he deemed to be the last time, it was with outbursts of ardent love that his heart went out to meet his Divine Lord.

He recalled then the promises he had made at his First Communion: how he had besought Jesus and Mary to be his constant friends, and resolved to prefer death rather than wilfully give way to sin. When his thanksgiving was over he said in complete tranquillity: "Now I am at peace; it is true that I have to make the long journey to eternity, but with our Divine Lord by my side, I have nothing to fear; tell everyone that if they have Him there is nothing to fear, not even death itself."

Dominic had always been a model of patience under suffering, but this virtue was even more conspicuous in him during his last illness, which he bore as a Saint. Whatever he could do for himself, he wished still to do, so as not to inconvenience anyone; he thought his parents had already had too much to bear from him. He took any and every medicine without the least sign of distaste, and underwent ten times the operation of blood letting without any sign of impatience.

After four days of attendance the doctor congratulated the boy and his parents on the improvement he found, and told the mother and father to thank God that now the worst was over, and only convalescence remained.

The parents were naturally pleased; but Dominic smiled and said: "The world is overcome. I have now only to make a befitting appearance before God."

When the doctor had gone, Dominic seemed to place no reliance on his promise of recovery, and asked that the Sacrament of Extreme Unction might be administered to him. In this again the parents only complied in order to satisfy him, for neither they nor the priest could perceive any signs of his being near to death; the very serenity of his countenance, and his bright conversation, made them believe that there was really some improvement.

But whether Dominic was guided by sentiments of devotion, or whether some divinely inspired voice had spoken to his heart, the fact is that he counted the days and hours of his life as a person reckons numbers in arithmetic, and every moment was occupied in preparation to appear before God. Before receiving Extreme Unction he expressed his devotion thus: "Pardon my sins, O God, for I love Thee, and wish to love Thee for ever! May this Sacrament which Thou permitted me to receive in Thy infinite mercy, blot out all the sins I have committed by my hearing, sight, tongue, hands and feet; may my body and soul be sanctified through the merits of Thy passion. Amen."

He answered all the responses in such a clear voice, and with such realisation of their meaning, that one would have imagined him to be in perfect health. It was then the 9th of March, the fourth day of his illness, and the last day of his life. His strength was diminishing, and remedies seemed to have no effect, so that the Papal Blessing was given. He said the Confiteor himself, and responded to the priest in his turn. When he was told that it earned with it a Plenary Indulgence, he showed the greatest joy and said Deo gratias et semper Deo gratias. Then he turned to the Crucifix and recited some verses of a favourite hymn.

Chapter XXIII

His Last Moments and Holy Death.

It is one of the maxims of our Faith that at the hour of death we reap the fruit of our good works during life: Quae seminaverit homo, haec et metet. However, it sometimes happens that good, pious people experience fear and dread at the approach of death. This is in accordance with the adorable decrees of God, who wishes to purify those souls from the small stains they may have contracted, so that they may increase their merit in heaven.

It was not thus with Dominic Savio. It is my conviction that God deigned to give him the hundredfold, which He bestows upon the souls of the just, as a preliminary to the glory of Paradise. And indeed the innocence which he preserved to the last moment of his life, his generous Faith, his habit of constant prayer, his mortifications, and the sufferings which had, as it were, beset his life, certainly merited that consolation for him at the hour of death.

Hence it was that he perceived his end approaching with the tranquillity of an innocent soul; it would seem that he did not feel even the suffering and oppressiveness which are a natural outcome of the efforts of the soul to break the bonds by which it is united to the body. In short, Savio's death was more like the passing into a peaceful slumber.

By the evening of March 9th he had received all the consolations of our Holy Religion. Anyone listening to his voice, or noticing his cheerful countenance, would have thought he was lying in bed for a little rest. His bright manner, his looks, still full of life, the complete possession of his senses, quite astonished everyone, and nobody, except himself, believed him to be on the point of death.

An hour and a half before he passed away, the parish priest came to see him, and seeing how calm he was, he was surprised to hear him recommending his soul to God. He continued to make aspirations and short ejaculations expressing his desire to go speedily to heaven.

The priest remarked: "I am at a loss to know what to suggest for the recommendation of a soul of this sort."

He recited some prayers, and was about to leave, when Dominic asked him for some final thought by way of souvenir. The priest said he could recommend nothing to him but the thought of the Sacred Passion; Dominic thanked him for this and continued to recall it, and to repeat invocations to Jesus and Mary. Then he rested for about half an hour.

At the end of that time he turned to his parents and said: "Father, it is time."

The father replied: "I am here, my son, what would you like?"

"It is time, father; get my prayer book, and read the prayers for a good death."

At these words the mother began to weep, and had to go out of the room. The father was greatly moved, but he restrained his grief so as to read the prayers. Dominic repeated them after him, and, in the proper place, said by himself: "Merciful Jesus, have mercy on me." When they came to the part which says: "But deign to receive me into Thy Kingdom where I may for ever sing Thy praises," Dominic added: "Yes, that is exactly what I desire; to sing the praises of God for all eternity." He now seemed to rest a moment, as though pondering over something in his mind. Then he opened his eyes again, and said with a clear voice, and a smiling countenance: "Goodbye, father, goodbye; the priest wanted to tell me something else, but I cannot remember it now . . . . Oh! what a beautiful sight I behold ...." Thus saying, with his hands joined, and a heavenly smile, his soul passed away.

Yes, go forth, faithful soul, to meet thy Creator; Heaven is opened to thee, and the angels and saints are rejoicing for thee; Jesus, whom you loved so much, invites you and says: "Come, good and faithful servant, thou hast fought and won the victory, come and enjoy that happiness which will never fail: Intra in gaudium Domini tui."

Chapter XXIV

The News of His Death. Remarkable Testimony.

The last words uttered by Dominic, as related in the preceding chapter, did not give his father the impression that he was dying, He thought he was again falling into a brief period of repose. He went out of the room for a few minutes, and on his return spoke to Dominic; but there was no reply, and he perceived that he had really expired. The grief of the parents and their desolation at the loss of such a son may be well imagined.

News was most anxiously awaited at the Oratory. A letter was dispatched to me in haste by his father, and when I read: "I have sad news for you," I concluded that all was over. He went on to say: "Our dear son, your pupil, gave up his soul to God yesterday evening, with the innocence of another St. Aloysius, and after receiving the Holy Sacrament in a most edifying manner."

There was consternation at the Oratory when I told the boys. Some were in grief at the loss of such a true friend; others, at being deprived of a valuable adviser, and all missed the inspiring example of his virtuous life. Some gathered together to say a prayer for him, but the greater number declared that they were sure he was a saint and already in Paradise. Some began immediately to invoke his intercession, and there was a general endeavour to get something that had belonged to him, as a relic. The master of the class that he attended in Turin, Father Picco, announced the sad tidings to his boys in these words:

"A short time ago, I happened to speak to you about the uncertainty of human life, and I pointed out that death does not spare even those who are in the spring time of youth. On that occasion, I had an example in one of the boys, who had been a pupil of this very class, a boy full of life and vigour, and yet after a few days absence we heard that he had been taken ill and had passed away, to the great sorrow of his parents and relations.

"When I brought forward that example I little thought that this year would be saddened by a similar occurrence, that such an instance would be repeated in the case of one who was sitting here listening to me. Death has carried off one of your companions, Dominic Savio. You may remember that he was not very well when he was here last, and then had to stay away from the classes altogether. The doctors advised his removal to his native place, and there he died after only four days of illness.

"Yesterday I read the letter from his father in which he makes the sad announcement, and the picture he draws of the boy's saintly death moved me to tears. He could find no more suitable expression to apply to his beloved son than to call him another St. Aloysius, both on account of the holiness of his life and his resignation in death. I leave to his superiors at the Oratory to describe the holiness of his life, the intensity of his fervour and piety; I must allow his companions and friends, who were in daily contact with him, to describe the gentleness and modesty of his demeanour, and the careful restraint he exercised over his words. As far as he came under my direction he always deserved the highest praise for his behaviour, his diligence and exactness, and it would afford me the greatest consolation if all of you would resolve to follow his example.

"While he was at the Oratory, but had not yet begun to attend these classes, his diligence and piety won for him the highest reputation. So rapid was his progress that I was most anxious for him to come, and I had the highest possible hopes for his future career. I had met him sometimes in my visits to the Oratory, had been struck by the innocence of his life and the winning gentleness of his disposition, and had been drawn to him in a particular manner. During the time that he attended these classes he fulfilled my expectations perfectly, and all of you are witnesses to his excellent conduct. In many details, which most boys consider beneath their notice, he was scrupulously exact, and by the fervour and recollection he brought to all his actions, he sanctified his whole day and made it an acceptable offering in the sight of God. Such conduct is worthy of imitation; it would bring consolation to parents and teachers, and all blessings and happiness to the boys themselves.

"Dominic gave us an example of how a life should be spent in the service of God, in contrast to those youths who seem to be in ignorance of the end for which they were created, or who stifle the good dispositions that come to every soul. Reflect on the example of Savio, and it will help you to spend your life in the service of your Creator and to be prepared to give an account when the time comes. If I notice an improvement in work and behaviour, I shall regard it as obtained by the intercession of Dominic, and as a reward for having been associated with him, if only for a short time."

Thus did Fr. Picco announce the death of one of his most promising pupils, and evince the general sorrow at his loss.

Chapter XXV

The Influence of Dominic's Virtues. Favours Received. A Recommendation.

Even after such a brief description of his life, it will not be surprising that God deigned to honour his servant, Dominic Savio, with special marks of honour, which made his virtues shine forth the brighter. During his life many had depended for guidance on his advice, and been encouraged by his example; others had recommended their intentions to his prayers, and they had often been answered in a striking manner. It was natural, therefore, that after his death confidence in his intercession should rapidly spread.

As soon as the news of his death reached us, many of his companions went about openly proclaiming him to be a saint. When the usual prayers were being offered for him, and the Litany was recited, they did not think it necessary or proper to say: "Pray for him" ;but continued the customary: "Pray for us." Dominic has gone to heaven, they said, and can need no payers from us.

Others said: "If Dominic, with his innocent life and good works, has not gone to Heaven, who will ever get there?" Thus it was that by degrees he became a regular model for the example of all, and was regarded as a powerful protector and intercessor in Heaven. Almost every day I received accounts of temporal and spiritual graces received. Illnesses were cured, sometimes immediately. I myself was a witness of an instantaneous cure of yellow fever. *

*This confidence in the intercession of Dominic was greatly increased by an assertion made is the strongest terms by his father. He says: "I was is the greatest affliction at the loss of my son, and was consumed by a desire to know what was his position in the other world. God deigned to comfort me. About a month after his death, during a very restless night, I saw, as it were, the ceiling opened, and Dominic appeared in the midst of dazzling light. I was beside myself at this sight, and cried out: "O Dominic, my son, are you already in Paradise?" "Yes," he replied, "I am in Heaven." Then pray for your brothers and sisters, and your mother and father, that we may all come to join you one day is Heaven." "Yes, yes, I will pray," was the answer. "Then he disappeared, and the room became as before." This the father asserts to be the simple truth.

I have before me many documents containing accounts of favours received through Dominic's intercession. The character and authority of the writers are beyond question; but as most of them are still alive, I shall not insert them for the present. There is one related here of a grace obtained by a student who had been a companion of Dominic's.

In the year 1858, this young man's health became very precarious. In fact it had broken down so badly, that he had to interrupt his course of philosophy, take every precaution, and at the end of the year he could not present himself for examination. However, there was a later examination towards the end of the year, and he thought he might be able to prepare for that, and thus prevent the loss of a whole year in the course of his studies; but his health continued to decline and his hopes gradually died away.

During the autumn vacation he had a change of air and rest, and this seemed to give him renewed strength, so that he returned to Turin and applied himself to his studies. But again his health broke down, and he was in a worse state than ever, so that he saw there was no possibility of application to study, or of taking an examination.

"It was then," he says, "that the accounts of the favours obtained by Dominic Savio struck me particularly, and I determined to make a novena to obtain the assistance of this former associate of mine. Certain prayers were said daily, and I made a special appeal on account of my previous intimacy with him, we having been in the same class, and striving for the first place.

"About the fifth day, my health was suddenly much better, and I immediately took to my books; I seemed to master the subjects with great ease and took the examination. Nor was it a short-lived favour, for my health has since remained perfect, and two months have now elapsed since I was ill. I cannot but recognise that this grace was obtained from God by the intercession of my companion and friend."

With this fact I shall bring the life of Dominic Savio to a close. In an appendix other favours are related, which seem to be conducive to the glory of God and the good of souls.

But, dear Reader, before parting, I should like to propose some little resolution, which may be of service to you and to myself and to others; I should like you to join with me to a resolution to imitate young Savio in the practice of the virtues which are compatible with our state. In his own position he lived a most happy, virtuous and innocent life, which was crowned by a holy death. If we imitate his manner of life, we shall be assured of being like him in our last moments.

But he is chiefly worthy of imitation in frequenting the Sacrament of Confession, which was his support in the constant practice of virtue, his guiding star through life, and his consolation at the hour of death. Frequent and devout use should be made of this sacrament so condusive to salvation; bbut every time we do so, let us give a thought to our last confession, in order to make sure that it has been properly made, and when there is need for so doing we should apply remedies to the defects. It seems to me that this is the safest means to spend happy days in the midst of the troubles of life, at the end of which we shall calmly await the moment of death.

Then, with our minds at rest, and a smile on our lips, we shall go forth to meet our Divine Lord who will graciously welcome us; and, judging us according to His great mercy, will lead us both, I trust, dear reader, from the trials of this life to a happy eternity.

Appendix

Certain Graces Obtained from God Through the Intercession of Dominic Savio.

Amongst the many graces which are attributed to the intercession of Dominic Savio I select some which are of a more ordinary nature.

Of these graces there exist at the Archiepiscopal Palace at Turin an authentic account, signed by the recipients of the heavenly favours, for the truth of which they have publicly vouched. In order that the account may be given with greater exactness and truthfulness, I have deemed it advisable to give the facts just as they are related in the authentic accounts above mentioned. They are as follows:

CURE OF A MALIGNANT FEVER.

If it be the duty of a Christian to keep hidden such facts as redound to his own honour, it is, on the other hand, his duty to manifest such things as serve to glorify God's servants and to exalt His Holy Name before men.

This duty it is that impels me to publish a fact concerning the servant of God, Dominic Savio, whom I recognise as my protector before God and the benefactor of my family.

I had recommended myself on several occasions to the pious Louis Comollo, as others had done, and God in His goodness had always answered my request; on many occasions also I recommended myself to Dominic Savio, and his intercession with Our Lord on my behalf was always efficacious. Private motives keep me from relating a number of facts; one however I must make known, both in order to give to God that honour which is His due, and to glorify before Christians the faithful servant, whom God Himself has deigned to make the depository of His treasures.

Here is the fact in question; in relating it I am only saying what is absolutely true, and conscientiously stated.

On the 8th September, 1858, I caught a severe chill, which after keeping me confined to my bed for some weeks, developed into fever.

I tried the various treatments prescribed by the doctors, but without avail. My delicate constitution and my weak state of health soon brought me to a state of great weakness and left me almost prostrate.

Visits from medical men, consultations, change of air, medicines, country, were all unavailing in my case. To my bodily ailments was added anxiety of mind, consequent on my inability to attend to my duty as a mother of a family. I was indeed unfortunate. Prostrate on a sick bed, all hopes in doctors and medicines gone, nothing now remained for me but help from Heaven, and this did not fail me. Only a few days before, a small book containing the life of Dominic Savio had been published, and moved by the virtues which he practised during life, and still more by the graces which others had obtained through his intercession, I resolved to recommend myself to him in order to obtain relief in my distress.

On the night, therefore, of February 20th, 1859, relying on the power of God, who grants His favours in abundance through the intercession of those who have been faithful to Him in life, urged on likewise by the need of comfort in my afflictions and relief in my infirmities, I gave utterance to the following words: "O thou, who in a few years of life didst attain to so high a degree of virtue, show forth the power and goodness of God; let me know that thou art in heaven and that from that happy place thou dost protect thy clients. Obtain from God that I may be relieved of my infirmities and may recover my former state of health. I promise that I will relate, whenever I am able, the favour which thou wilt obtain for me from God." I had hardly finished these last words, when I felt a sort of shivering through my whole body. I felt at once a great relief; my infirmities vanished, the fever disappeared and a sweet sleep stole upon me, so that I was able to spend that night in calm repose. In the morning I was perfectly cured.

Dr. Frola, who came to see me, was not a little astonished at so great an improvement. "I do not know," he said, "what remedy has been able to do you so much good. Certainly the finger of God has been here."

I got up from my bed and found myself in perfect health, after a sickness which should have required some months at least of convalescence.

Eight months have elapsed since my cure, and up to the present, thank God, through the intercession of that holy youth, Dominic Savio, I have not been subject to ailments of any sort. All this that I have of my own accord here set down, I desire to be published wherever it may be deemed to promote the greater glory of God and the good of souls: and I am prepared to testify to the truth of the same in the presence of any person whatsoever. I have subsequently on various occasions had recourse to this heavenly benefactor and have always been heard. May these facts serve to strengthen the faith of other faithful Christians, so that they may have recourse to this source of blessings; and may they find in their spiritual and temporal needs effectual help in him, who lived a holy life on earth, and now in his glory protects us from heaven.

COUNTESS BUSCHETTI
née di Mazzenile.
(Turin, 15 October, 1859.)

CURE OF A SERIOUS EYE COMPLAINT.

It was in 1858, about the end of May, that my eyes became seriously affected, and the pain continued, sometimes diminishing, sometimes increasing, up to the November of 1859. Beginning from the month of March of that year it increased to such an extent that I was from the very outset constrained to lay aside all studies, and later on to give them up altogether. In the early part of July my affliction had increased to such an extent, that college life, which I had before enjoyed, now appeared to me to be unbearable.

Thus it came about, that, owing to the state of my eyes, and the regret I felt at the sight of my companions working for the approaching examinations, I had to go home: I thought some improvement might follow, and indeed I did get slightly better, but only for a short time. Four or five days had scarcely elapsed from the time the improvement set in, when the malady again took a turn for the worse, and I was not merely reduced to my former state, but to a far more deplorable one. I then had recourse to several doctors. One of them required me to take about 400 pills of some particular make; I took them as prescribed and followed minutely the directions given me, but all to no effect. I was bled four times, but without avail. On five occasions I submitted to blistering operations behind the ears without deriving any benefit thereby. I was at this time visited by other well known eye specialists, amongst others Cavaliere Sperim, Dr. Fissore and Dr. Paganini, but, after submitting me to various tests, they told me plainly that the way to cure the disease with which I was afflicted was still to them an unknown problem.

Weary, then, at my hopeless plight I knew not where to turn. My days were spent continually in a dark room. All amusement was a source of horror to me and my eyes had become abnormally inflamed. Towards the end of October I seemed to feel some improvement, and, with the hope of a speedy and complete cure l returned to the college. A fortnight, however, had hardly elapsed when my eyes again began to give me so much trouble that I felt doubtful of ever being able to study again. I then had my arms blistered and the operation was subsequently repeated; the same was done several times to my ears, but no benefit resulted. I often spoke to the Director of the House about it, and he, in order to console me, would address to me such words as he knew would be to my temporal and spiritual advantage, encouraging me to be patient, and holding out hopes of a speedy recovery.

One evening, whilst all the boys were engaged in some singing classes, I was sitting thoughtful and sad, with my face buried in my hands, and leaning on the table near which the Director was seated. Presently he arose, and coming quietly up to me, touched me on the shoulder, smiling as he did so, and spoke to me as follows: "Why can we not free you, once and for all, from this trouble? I wish to see the end of it. Let us endeavour to take possession of Dominic Savio and not allow him to depart until he has obtained your cure?" At these words I looked at him steadfastly, but said nothing. Then he continued: "Yes, pray every day during this novena (it was the eve of the first day of the novena for the feast of the Immaculate Conception) to Dominic Savio, that he may intercede for you. Endeavour to be in such a state as to be able to go to Communion every day of this novena. In the evening, before retiring to bed, say these words: "Dominic Savio, pray for me," and add one 'Hail Mary.' " I promised to do this exactly, upon which he continued: "That is right, do what I have told you and I will remember you every day of this novena in the Holy Mass." "And who knows," he added, "whether this time Dominic Savio will succeed in escaping us before you have been cured."

On the very day that I began to make the novena I felt an improvement in my malady. I then continued the practices of piety with greater fervour, and was soon rewarded for doing so, for in a few days my eyes were completely cured. During the novena I had promised that, if, after a certain time, I had no further relapse, I would do my best to have published, in honour of Dominic Savio, the grace I had received from him.

I now keep my promise, for the time fixed (1st February, 1860) has elapsed and I am in perfect health. I hope that Dominic Savio will continue to bestow his favours upon me, and I on my part shall do all that I can to show my gratitude to him, striving to imitate him in those virtues of which he gave such a striking example. Meanwhile let praise be rendered to God and to Dominic Savio, through whose special protection I obtained this grace.

(Turin, 1st February, 1860).

Thank God, my eyes are still in a perfectly healthy condition, and I hereby confirm the above statement.

EDWARD DONATA, of Saluggla.
(Turin, March 20th, 1861).

INSTANTANEOUS CURE OF TOOTHACHE.

Having read the life of the holy youth Dominic Savio I conceived a deep veneration for him.

But a fact worthy of notice?a fact which has made me deeply indebted to this heavenly Protector, is the one I am about to set down, with the request that you will give it that publicity which you may think fit. On the morning of Thursday, the 7th of April of the present year (1859) I had a slight attack of headache. I paid no heed to it, thinking it was only a passing indisposition, but it increased as the day went on, so that I was unable to work or to sleep the following night. On getting up on Friday, with the pain ever increasing, I was seized with such a sharp attack of toothache that although I went to class I could neither study nor attend to the explanations given, nor to anything else, so severe was the pain I experienced. The trouble went on increasing until, in the evening, in sheer desperation, I was seized with a fit of uncontrollable weeping. It was time for the evening class and I was wandering aimlessly about the house, a prey to racking pain, when the prefect met me on the balcony overlooking the playground. "Recommend yourself to Dominic Savio," he said to me, for he understood the cause of my trouble. "Recommend yourself to Dominic Savio; he can cure you if he wishes to do so." I thanked him for this advice and reproached myself for not having thought about it sooner. I hastened at once to Our Lady's altar, knelt down on the step which had so often been hallowed by the presence of Savio, when he used to withdraw to the silence of the sanctuary, his heart filled with devotion towards her, by whose aid he succeeded in attaining the love, zeal and piety which now form a crown of glory for him in heaven.

Kneeling down there I made the sign of the Cross and began to pray, determined, at any cost, to obtain my cure, provided it were in accordance with the will of God. The pain was then at its worst, but at the moment I was saying the words: "Sed libera nos a malo," the aching pain suddenly ceased. My blood resumed its usual course, the face assumed its natural proportions and I found myself cured and at ease, without any trace remaining to remind me of the agony I had suffered. How can I express the gratitude I then felt, and will ever feel, towards young Savio! What esteem do I not furthermore owe to him, who so speedily cured my body, for the good done to my soul!

I beg you to take this account into consideration, and make use of it in such a manner as you may judge most suited to promote the glory of God, and confidence in the holy youth Dominic Savio.

Obediently yours,

MATTHEW GALLEANO, of Caramangna

THE TESTIMONY OF A MOTHER CONCERNING HER SON'S CURE.

My only son had been lying sick in the hospital of SS. Maurice and Lazarus for nearly a month. The cause of his illness was a rush of blood to the brain, which made him delirious. Amongst other circumstances of his illness, one deserving of special remark was that nothing could make him utter a word. No one can imagine the sorrow of a mother who beholds heir only son a prey to a disease which shows no hope of being cured. In my advanced years I should have been left without help of any kind, and my life, in consequence would have been a most unhappy one.

One day, when under the weight of the deepest sorrow, I went with some relatives to the hospital. Whilst we were by the patient's bed, I heard how many times he had been bled, and at the sight of the death-like pallor and emaciation of his features, I burst into tears and nothing seemed able to console me. But thanks be to God, Who deigned to comfort me in an unexpected manner and to change my sorrow into the greatest consolation! Some little distance off I noticed a young man with a small book in his hands; he went to a bed next to the one where my son was lying, and having opened the book, showed to the patient a picture of a boy about fifteen years of age, whose virtuous life was related in the book. He advised the patient to read and to imitate the virtues of the boy who lived and died like a saint. At the sight of the book and the picture I thought at once that the boy represented in it was some saint, and approaching, I said to the one who held the book in his hands, "for the love of God and of Our Blessed Lady give me one of those books for my son." He answered that he would willingly do so, but that it would be useless to give it to one in delirium to read, and that it would be better for him to recommend himself to Domiriic Savio, imploring him to obtain his cure. I at once approved of the proposal, and going close to my son I said to him in a faltering voice: "My son; listen, recommend yourself to Dominic Savio so that he may obtain your cure from God." At these words he turned towards me, but remained for a few moments motionless. Then suddenly, to the great surprise of those standing by and to my great consolation he said: "I recommend myself to him." Words will not express the joy and satisfaction which my heart experienced on hearing the voice of a son, whose cure I had almost despaired of, on hearing that voice which for eighteen days had not sounded in my ears. I then endeavoured to make him understand the holiness and virtues of Savio, to whom we had both earnestly appealed.

Shortly afterwards there was a complete change, and he was entirely cured from a disease which the doctors declared could only end in death or the asylum.

MARY PAIRA.
(Turin, April 10th, 1860).

SUDDEN CURE OF RUPTURE.

Amongst other favours obtained after recourse to Dominic Savio, the wonderful cure of a young student deserves to be recorded. I, myself and many others were witnesses of this fact, which is here described by the recipient of the favour.

Three years ago I suffered from rupture, and though cured of it, I had undergone intense pain on that account. But on February 20th of this year (1860), I was attacked by the same complaint whilst at recreation in the playground. I could not stand and was put to bed suffering intensely. The doctor was sent for, and at his advice, everything was prepared for another operation; a carriage was sent for to convey me to the hospital. The pain I was suffering at this time was too great to bear, and a sort of delirium took possession of me; some thought, in fact, that I was surely dying.

But it was just then that I thought of our deceased companion, Dominic Savio. I had read his life and knew all about the favours he had obtained, so I appealed to him, saying: "If it be true that you are in heaven, obtain some relief for me in this illness." I then recited in his honour an Our Father, Hail Mary, and Glory be to the Father.

I had scarcely finished the prayers, when a peaceful calm came over me, and brought on a refreshing, sleep. But after a short time, I was awakened by those who had been sent for to take me to the hospital. To their surprise I said: "My pain has all gone." They found that I was perfectly cured, and had it not been growing late, I should have got up again from bed. However, on the following morning all traces of my attack had disappeared, and I arose with the others in the best of health.

I desire to offer my tribute of deep gratitude to this faithful Servant of God.

CHARLES BELLINO (Aosta).

A Double Cure

The Very Rev. Don Rua, the first successor of Don Bosco, gives the following account:

A signal favour was obtained through the intercession of Dominic Savio in the town of Chieri. A man, named Charles Bechio, had suffered for three years with a very serious rupture. He could not apply himself to any work, for as soon as he made the slightest effort, the pain became so acute that he could not stand on his feet. He had already applied all the remedies suggested by doctors and surgeons, but the illness only increased.

At the beginning of this year he chanced to read the life of Dominic Savio, and learning that many sick people had been cured by him, even instantaneously, he felt his faith and confidence revive, and hoped to be favoured in the same way. He began a novena at once for this end, and promised that if he were cured, he would go to Don Bosco to attest the fact. In the very beginning of the novena he noticed that his pains were diminishing, and an improvement had set in. After three days he put aside his truss, and by the end of the novena was perfectly cured, so that he could again undertake his work, which was of a very vigorous and tiring nature. It was then the month of March, and from that time has not been in the slightest pain.

Moreover, Dominic did not only obtain for him this temporal favour, but a spiritual one as well, of greater consequence. For some years he had not approached the Sacrament of Penance, and felt such a repugnance to do so, that nothing but a special grace would have been able to conquer it. Accordingly he had recommended this intention also to Dominic, and when his novena was over, all his old repugnance and hesitation disappeared, and he felt a desire of drawing near to God. In fact he approached the Sacraments of Penance and Holy Communion to his great consolation.

The undersigned has taken this down from the recipient of the grace, who is ready to make any attestation required.

MICHAEL RUA (Priest).
(Turin, March 10th. 1861).

Cure of a Serious Affliction of the Eyes

A matter of great importance urges me to write to you. During January of this year, I had been troubled with a painful malady of the eyes, and having tried all material remedies in vain, I determined to have recourse to a spiritual one. Remembering your former pupil, Dominic Savio, and the many graces obtained. for those who invoked his intercession, I had recourse to him also. It was on January 19th, and whilst in the act of prayer, it seemed that he bathed my eyes in some miraculous manner, and from that moment the pain ceased and my sight became quite clear and strong.

It is my earnest wish that the foregoing should be added to the accounts of other miracles worked by God for the glory of his servant.

LAURENCE PELAZZA.
(Carmagnola, April 1861).

A Dangerous Illness Overcome

Having been requested by a number of prudent persons to inform you of a cure obtained through the intercession of Dominic Savio, I would ask you to add it to the other accounts sent to you.

In July 1871, I was attacked by such a violent cough that I could get no rest either night or day. The doctor was sent for, and he consulted others, but there was no sign of improvement. After some days I was evidently growing weaker and was troubled with catarrh, which made breathing impossible. Acute bronchitis set in. I was unable to do anything but a little reading, and so I picked up Dominic Savio's life, although it was already familar to me.

His virtuous life, and the favours he had obtained, naturally suggested to me that I should have recourse to him in my illness, and I began a triduum or three days of prayer. When the doctor came next he found such a marked improvement, that he said it could not be due to human aid or power. "It seems like an illusion," he said. The cough that had been racking me for three months was gone, together with the bronchitis which was slowly wearing me away; now, instead, I go about with sound and robust health, blessing Savio for obtaining such a signal favour.

J. B. PELLEGRINI (COMO).

Such is the Ven. Don Bosco's narrative of the Life of Dominic Savio, and of some of the favours obtained through his intercession. These favours have been multiplied in the years that have passed; they have been influential in the progress of the Cause of his Canonisation, which was formally introduced at Rome in February last (1914). Much has been written about Dominic Savio, particularly since that event, but we may well conclude by giving the Reader the words of His Eminence the late Cardinal Parocchi, who wrote in 1895: "May the young learn from Savio how to sanctify themselves, even in the midst of dangers, how to join holiness with cheerfulness, frankness with reserve, dignity with modesty, the interior life and intimate union with Our Lord with the diligent exercise of external duties; let them learn of him to be beloved by God and men, and thus to leave a holy memory to succeeding generations."

FINIS.

Made in the USA
San Bernardino,
CA